## Growing Up Poor in London

'A good reporter's book in its clarity, precision and style, but it is in addition a work of perception and warmth such as few reporters could achieve' *Illustrated London News*

'Exceptionally readable . . . a valuable social document' *The Times*

'Louis Heren's fascinating memoir of his childhood and adolescence and on the now almost extinct London in which he grew up. Lovingly, and in meticulous detail, he transmutes his thoughts and feelings as a child with the imaginative insight of a good poet or novelist . . . I shall mainly think of it as a kind of urban *Cider with Rosie:* there is a similar affectionate, perceptive, sometimes mildly sentimental, sometimes funny, always honest recreation of a boy's life in a particular place' *New Statesman*

'Splendidly written, full of interest, humour and humanity' *Bookseller*

'. . . the variety, the spice, of the life he describes, with its simple flavour of delight in simple pleasures' *Daily Telegraph*

The late Louis Heren was born the youngest of three children in Shadwell, a slum parish in the East End of London, in 1919. His father, who had been a printer on *The Times,* died when he was four, leaving his mother to run the City of Dublin Dining Rooms opposite the West Garden Gate of London Docks; *A Good Pull Up For Carmen,* it said in one window, and *T.G.W.U. United We Stand Divided We Fall* in the other. It was always the ambition of 'our mother', as the author calls her, that Louis should follow his father to Printing House Square, which he did, starting as a messenger boy and finally retiring as Deputy Editor and Foreign Editor in 1981. Along the way he served as the paper's correspondent in India, Israel and the Middle East, South-east Asia and Washington.

*By Louis Heren*

The New American Commonwealth
No Hail, No Farewell
Growing Up on *The Times*
Growing Up Poor in London

# LOUIS HEREN

# Growing Up Poor
# in London

PHŒNIX

To Our Mother
who thought that this book should have been entitled
*Growing Up with the Poor in London*

A PHOENIX PAPERBACK

First published in Great Britain in 1973
by Hamish Hamilton Ltd
This paperback edition first published in 1996
by Indigo

Reissued in 2001 by Phoenix,
an imprint of Orion Books Ltd,
Orion House, 5 Upper St Martin's Lane,
London WC2H 9EA

Copyright © 1973 Louis Heren
Introduction © 1995 Peter Hennessy

The right of Louis Heren to be identified as the author
of this work has been asserted by him in accordance
with the Copyright, Designs and Patents Act 1988.

A CIP catalogue record for this book
is available from the British Library

ISBN 0 75381 251 7

Printed and bound in Great Britain by
The Guernsey Press Co. Ltd,
Guernsey, C.I.

# Introduction

Louis Heren fills these pages in the way that he once filled a room — with presence, depth, humanity and, above all, warmth. Yet, like Irish coffee, his was always a warmth tempered by bite. The distinctive tang of his personality (the product of his special formation, something of which is captured in this volume) meant that his ability to converse easily and affably with anyone about almost anything could suddenly give way to a blunt directness. A dash of the false, the pretentious or the patronizing could produce a swift weather-change across that wonderfully expressive face. The result would be pure *old* dockland in language, idiom and accent. For the East End of London had made him, and, as Louis put it himself, he 'never shook off Shadwell and my Cockneyness'.

As a young, Cambridge-honed journalist on *The Times*, I experienced his abrasive side every few months, especially if he thought I had missed the point of a story, or I thought his populism was getting the better of him. We would engage in a volley of fierce exchanges, the verbal equivalent of Centre Court at Wimbledon. Then the Heren grin would suffuse his countenance and I would be despatched back to my room with an affectionate expletive. Louis was a bruiser who left no bruises – a great gift in a newspaper man.

As a boss he was a treat, an inspiration and an instructor *par excellence*. For with his stocky frame and his muscular, no-nonsense mind he was the incarnation of that mid-century

British generation of 'temporary gentlemen', recruited to the wartime officer class without the benefit of public school or university grooming on the way, a generation which left such an impression on post-war public and political life. The best of them, like Louis, had fire in their bellies and compassion in their hearts.

Without the shock of Hitler, that stuffed-up inter-war British society would never have dropped the kind of ladders which enabled a bright kid from Shadwell to rise up to become a man of Louis' eminence and influence. He would not thank me for saying so, but what a travesty it was, as well as a downright injustice, that Louis was not appointed Editor of *The Times*, to see the paper he had joined as a messenger boy in 1934 through its bumpy transition from the Thompsons' ownership to its acquisition by the Murdoch empire in 1981.

This, however, is very definitely *not* a book of might-have-beens. It's a study of life as it was by a superb natural storyteller who lived in that great working-class hinterland around the London Docks, in what turned out to be the last days of Britain's seaborne empire. Its pages are corrugated by the texture of life in those singular urban villages (and Louis was an urban villager to his fingertips). The smell and feel of twenties and thirties Shadwell seep out of Louis' paragraphs like a November mist slinking up and away from the Thames.

But *Growing Up Poor* is not just a choice confection of vignettes of an East End community now lost. There are rich pickings here for the historian which range wider than his firsthand account of Cable Street when the East End saw off Mosley's fascists. His description of the sheer coping capacity of his widowed mother running her City of Dublin Dining Rooms near the West Garden Gate of the docks is magnificent in every sense. And his depiction of her world view is a fine encapsulation of the working-class patriotism which shaped

Louis himself so powerfully: 'For her patriotism was personal. She believed in the monarchy, the church and the Empire because she saw herself as part of it.'

There was a strong echo in Louis Heren, too, of the great dockers' leader Ernest Bevin, particularly of what Bevin called 'the poverty of the aspirations' of 'my people'. This is heard strongly in an especially rich chapter in *Growing Up Poor* about life and attitudes in the self-consciously proletarian 2nd City of London Sea Scouts. Louis' friend Kelly was the incarnation of such meagre ambitions. He combined wit and poverty in equal measure, 'summed up the best and worst of Cockney life; the fortitude, the humour and the sticking-together and the basic pessimism and rejection of ambition'.

Come to think of it, Louis *was* the Ernie Bevin of the post-war *Times* – fiercely loyal to his staff and robust in his views and argument; four-square and patriotic in his attitudes; well-primed on international affairs but never forgetful of the condition of the people back home in all his years as a foreign correspondent. And he was the very best man to have around when the troubles started arriving in battalions. Like Bevin, Louis was a turn-up-in-a-million, and the conditions which made him so can never be replicated. This book explains why.

I knew *Growing Up Poor* was a classic when I first read it. I know it remains a classic today. For the book was the man and the man, as near as one person could be, was the inter-war East End.

PETER HENNESSY
Walthamstow
*Boxing Day, 1995*

# 1

I WAS BORN in Shadwell, a slum parish in the East End of London, on 6 February, 1919. I was the youngest of three children, and our father died when I was four years old. Our mother did not marry again, although she was only in her early thirties, and for many years was not entitled to a widow's pension. I grew up in the depression years when men were lucky if they got two or three half-day's work a week in the docks. The dole, or unemployment pay, did not provide for subsistance living. The weekly allowance for children was one shilling, the then price of 20 Gold Flake cigarettes. Nearly everybody was poorly clothed and ill-fed. The tenements and little terraced cottages were old and crowded. In some tenements, or buildings as we called them, many families shared one lavatory. The unemployed and under-employed hung about at street corners, and often got fighting drunk on Saturday nights. Beer was fourpence a pint. Many of the women, generally dressed in black pinafores, coarse aprons, woollen shawls and men's caps, worked in the City as chars. They would join their men in the pubs on Friday or Saturday night, often carrying babies, while the older children stood outside eating penny sponge cakes or arrowroot biscuits which most pubs kept in big glass bottles behind the bar.

It ought to have been a wretched life, but it wasn't. At least not for us. Our mother ran a coffee shop, not the fancy kind which sprang up all over London after the second world war, but what was known as *A Good Pull Up for Carmen*. She did not make much money, but we never went hungry. I can't remember wearing an overcoat before I went to work, but was always decently dressed. We were lucky. We were not so well off as the publicans and some of the shopkeepers, but were better off than most. Our mother kept the world at a distance—or kept herself to herself, as she would say—but we were part of the neighbourhood. It was a friendly place in spite of the poverty, the dock walls, and heavy traffic. We had friends and many acquaintances, and played in the streets which were entirely safe. There was always much to do. Few toffs could have had such a crowded calendar. Life was nearly always absorbing and often exciting. I never felt poor or deprived.

Shadwell was not a homogeneous neighbourhood. The native-born Cockneys were certainly a minority, and the majority were immigrants, mainly Irish Catholics and Polish Jews. Some African and West Indian seamen had married local women and settled down. One of the ropes, or lodging houses, was home for Indian pedlars, Sikhs who hawked garish scarves and shawls in the poorer districts of London. I can still smell the curry from the underground communal kitchen where they cooked their evening meals. The rope was next to a pub, the *Gunboat*, which was used by the Irish. There was no racial violence, but religious prejudice was intense throughout the neighbourhood. I suppose that we were all anti-Semitic because we knew that the Jews had killed Jesus. Many of our Jewish neighbours spoke only Polish and Yiddish. The beards and side-curls of the Orthodox were absolutely foreign, and their demeanour occasionally frightening. In retrospect I have wondered if those Jews realized how alien they were, and why they did not try to meet us halfway, but prejudice never led to physical violence. Apart from the Jews, the mutual antipathies of the Catholics and Protestants were constant, and the Nonconformists hardly ever spoke to anyone. They were a kind of Christian Jews in that they assumed an unspoken superiority over others. They also separated themselves. They went to chapel and not to church. They were supposed not to smoke or drink, and were said to be mean. A man could be dying outside their chapel, our mother used to say, and they would not give him the smell of an oil rag.

Yet we all lived peacefully alongside each other if not together. We were all poor, including the Jews who worked in the tailoring sweatshops. The Irish had a song with the refrain, *No Jews allowed down Wapping*, but sang it without provocation. I was a Sabbath *Goy*, and earned a few pennies lighting fires for the Orthodox on Friday evenings. My first sweetheart was Jewish, a slight girl with grey eyes named Helen. The courtship did not last long. I was shy, but there was also the unspoken but accepted religious prohibition. Nevertheless, Mr Wolvewitch who kept the bootshop down the street was kind and used to wish us a Merry Christmas. We knew that Passover was a great religious holiday. St Patrick's Day was celebrated by everybody, except possibly by the Nonconformists. I went to school with a bunch of shamrock pinned to my jersey and lots of kids wore the green.

Canon Ring of the Catholic church of St Mary and St Michael in the Commercial Road was a power in the neighbourhood. The general understanding was that he was well known in the Vatican and Downing Street, and men of all faiths touched their caps when he stalked by. The annual Catholic street procession, held I suppose on the feast of St Mary and St Michael, was a great occasion. The Catholics put up little altars draped with lace curtaining and bedsheets outside their houses and scrubbed the pavement. White clothes and shoes were bought for the children. The High Street cut across all the main approaches to the London Docks, but traffic stopped while the various sodalities walked in procession carrying banners, statues and lighted candles. The children sang their *Aves*, and watching from the pavement I would feel envious because they seemed possessed by a special grace. Protestant ire would rise when the men went by singing *Faith of Our Fathers* (the hymn of the Catholic resistance?) and *God Bless Our Pope*. We all knew about scheming Rome and hated Popery, but would almost stand to attention when the Canon passed carried on a litter under a canopy, dressed in gorgeous vestments and blessing Catholic, Protestant, Jew and Nonconformist alike. Prejudice as well as poverty lurked behind most lace curtains, but there was almost always a certain civility in the streets.

A great unifying force for many was politics, international, national and local, but especially national. The election results proved the almost unbelievable fact that some Tories lived in the neighbourhood but the overwhelming majority, regardless of religion and origin, voted Labour. Differences were hidden under the flag of the party, and in those days in Shadwell it was very red. I knew the words of the *Red Flag* and the *Internationale* when I was still in elementary school. (I can remember singing the *Internationale* in German with two Special Branch men and Malcolm Muggeridge late one night in the garden of King's House, the British High Commissioner's residence, in Kuala Lumpur during the Malayan war in the fifties, but that's another story.) Poverty did not make Shadwell a hotbed of revolution. Communists were remarkably few, but I think that the idea was widespread that through politics we could make a better world. This was almost a religious belief for some of us. The *Internationale* with its refrain *So comrades let's rally, and the last great fight let us face*, was as inspiring as *Onward Christian Soldiers*, which we also sang.

Elections were emotional occasions. I rang my first doorbells and distributed leaflets when I was very young. The comings and goings of the candidates were events, especially on election nights, and processions would march to the Town Hall in Cable Street. I can remember a rich Tory candidate calling at the shop, I think he was a Guinness, and our mother serving him tea. The candidate's wife was very beautiful and self-assured, but no more than our mother. She presided over the blue enamel pot as if it was Queen Anne silver, and I think I then had the first intimation of her bourgeois ambitions for us. I also suspected that she was a Tory at heart, although only Labour posters were displayed in the shop windows. I was wrong.

She was truly egalitarian, and could not conceive that she was inferior to anybody—or superior, with the possible exception of Catholics, Jews, Nonconformists and foreigners. She had a strong radical streak. Years afterwards, when I was home on leave from Washington, I drove her to see my brother who had moved to Huntingdonshire. Going home was a longish night drive, and as Cockneys will we sang. We all joined in the usual medley of old and new songs, and my American-educated children sang *Marching through Georgia*. Our mother had her own refrain which went: *Why should we be beggars with ballots in our hands, When God gave the land to the people*. We were proud of our radical and egalitarian views although we may not have recognized them as such. I was possibly dim, but was unaware of the British class system until I went to Sandhurst during the second world war as an officer cadet and temporary gentleman.

Politics was an abiding interest in our family. We read the old *News Chronicle* in the morning and the *Star* in the evening, and always listened to the B.B.C. news and public affairs programmes. I can remember listening to Commander Stephen King Hall on the children's programme, on Fridays I think, and to the gravelly voice of Raymond Gram Swing explaining the mysteries of Congress from Washington. Alistair Cooke also broadcast from New York a series of American work and folk songs recorded by some W.P.A. team. I now trace my interest in the United States back to those broadcasts, but then the bitter songs of protest were heard as reassuring evidence of what we supposed was a trans-Atlantic workers' solidarity. We read of John L. Lewis with patriotic pride—he was born in Wales—and were excited by the Reuther brothers closing down the automobile plants in Detroit with their sit-down strikes. Roosevelt was a hero, and the nine old men of the U.S. Supreme Court were worse than the Inquisition.

We followed other foreign events, especially the rise of Hitler and the Spanish civil war. I read Tom Wintringham in the *Chronicle*, and assumed that I would join the International Brigade as soon as I grew up. But these events were nearly always related to our condition in Shadwell, and national and trade union politics were our first concern. Ernest Bevin was another hero, and I can remember him haranguing a crowd of striking dock workers outside the Town Hall. Somehow I always associated him with the Tolpuddle Martyrs, presumably because he came from the West Country. For reasons long forgotten, we had a low opinion of Herbert Morrison although he was a fellow Cockney. He was then in local politics, and our religious and ethnic snobberies might have explained the antipathy. We were suspicious of most local politics because of the feeling that the Irish had more than their fair share of influence at the Town Hall. One of their leaders, Sullivan by name, was in fact an effective and reforming politician. He was a big handsome man, as Irishmen are supposed to be, who could dominate or charm a crowd. He was responsible for one of the first slum-clearance schemes in the neighbourhood, but blocks of flats were built in Wapping, the Irish redoubt, which persuaded our mother that the Irish looked only after their own. We believed her of course.

Shadwell was in the borough then known as Stepney which has since become part of Tower Hamlets. The new name is appropriate because although the many neighbourhoods and parishes merged into one another each had the separate characteristics of a hamlet. Shadwell, or Shadywell, was a riverside hamlet hundreds of years before the docks were dug and its boundaries disappeared in the early Victorian urban sprawl. Many of the original Cockneys looked to the river for their livelihood, where they were employed aboard tugboats, lighters and sailing barges. Those who worked in the docks were generally stevedores. The dockers, or un-skilled labour, were almost entirely Irish. There was always talk about tides and winds, and a tide table hung prominently in the shop. Of an evening the riverside pubs and the New Park were filled with people watching the traffic go by, the Russian boats bound for Hays Wharf, the General Steam Navigation ships dropping down from their moorings at the Customs House, and trim little coasters homeward bound for Holland and Germany.

We children were also drawn to the river, and at low tide played on the beaches below the old waterman's steps between the warehouses. We used to swim in the river in spite of the river police patrolling in their black launches and the occasional dead rat floating by. I can still see, at watery eye-level, their exposed pink bellies. I could see the masts and the black and green funnels of the Irish boats from my bedroom window, and at night listened to the sirens of ships moving on the river. Now they reverberate through my mind like concentrated nostalgia; then they were always sad but promised adventure. There was a preface or first chapter in one of H. M. Tomlinson's books—*Gallion's Reach*, I think—about a ship coming up the river after months at sea which I read and re-read. I always assumed I would be a sailor.

Thus Shadwell was not just another industrial slum which had grown up round a factory. The river, the London River as the watermen always called the Thames, made all the difference. Many of the orginal Cockneys had deep roots in the parish. Some rarely went beyond its unmarked boundaries, except when working on the river or for trips to Southend, Epping Forest and Hampstead Heath, and I always knew when I crossed them. West of Dellow Street was the parish of St George-in-the-East, which stretched to the Tower. North of Cable Street was the Commercial Road and Whitechapel, and mainly Jewish. It had no attractions except when stars such as Sophie Tucker played at the local music hall. We all knew the words of *My Yiddisher Mama*. Beyond the New Park and well to the east was Limehouse where we never went but knew to be filled with Chinese tong men and opium dens. (We read in the *News of the World* of beautiful young society girls becoming addicts there, just as in du Maurier's *Trilby*.) To the south were the river and the docks, and across the dock bridges and lockgates was the man-made island of Wapping which again was rarely visited because of the Irish.

Within these boundaries Shadwell was still very much a village or hamlet, as self-conscious and for us as isolated as if it was surrounded by fields instead of other slums and the river. The parish church of St Paul's was our village centre.

On Sundays I sang in the choir at Matins and Evensong, and went to Sunday school. I served on the altar at the 7 a.m. Holy Communion Service on Wednesdays, and attended two choir practices every week except in August. A variety of clubs met in the church hall. The big churchyard was a wonderful place to play in, as was the crypt with its broken coffins. The garden fete was the event of the summer. The vicarage was as imposingly big as any to be found in the country, and it had a lovely but unkempt garden running down to the river and the entrance to the docks. There was more than one rector during my childhood, but in memory they have merged into one image of a withdrawn, kindly man with a cultivated voice. He wore a Military Cross on his vestments with his first world war medals, and generally behaved as a military chaplain taking care of the troops. We were proud of the M.C., the accent and the suggestion of high living, although in his own way he must have been desperately poor. We felt a social superiority over the Catholics, in spite of the formidable presence of Canon Ring, because we belonged to the Church Established along with the King and Queen.

To that extent, life was not so very different from that of children better off or living in a rural village. We had much the same pastimes, and played cricket and football on cinder pitches in the New Park as well as the asphalt school play-ground and the street. On balance, we were probably better off than ordinary country children. The schools and the local Carnegie library were very good, and of course there was London which we roamed as far as the museums in Exhibition Road. Our mother used to make up sandwiches and give us fourpence for the Underground fare to South Kensington, but we would pocket the money and ride free on the backs of lorries and the few remaining horse-drawn

17

carts. The science and natural history museums were the favourites but we also wandered through the Victoria and Albert. At Christmas our mother took us to the pantomime at the Lyceum theatre and afterwards to the Lyons Corner House in the Strand for high tea. She liked musical comedies, and I can recall lining up for the pit of the Coliseum to see *White Horse Inn* and at Daly's for the *Duchess of Danzig*. At the time, these rather foolish but nice productions appeared to be the best theatre. I did not know of course that I was just captivated by the theatre, the assumed mystery of make-believe, but soon afterwards I discovered the Old Vic and Sadlers Wells, and got to know Shakespeare, opera—mainly Italian but some Mozart and Gounod's *Faust*—and ballet.

In summer our mother took us to Hastings for two weeks, and during the rest of the summer holiday we regularly walked through Rotherhithe Tunnel under the river to Southwark to swim in the open-air pool in the park there for twopence. The pavement through the tunnel was narrow, and we used to walk in single file with heavy lorries thundering by. The smell and dust were awful. We were always dirty when we got home again carrying our wet swimsuits and towels, but the park was lovely and the pool fascinating with girls in two-piece suits. The walk through the tunnel was also an adventure. For me at least, London changed south of the river—or over the water as our mother used to say. The Surrey Docks were used by boats bringing timber from the Baltic. There were hardly any Jews and few Irish. Oddly enough, the difference for me was made apparent by the Scandinavian church by the exit of the tunnel. I was to recognize this distinctive architecture years afterwards in Copenhagen, but then it was just south of the river.

The Oxbridge undergraduates at the church and the local settlement house pitied us for growing up in such an environment. The fact that I was an orphan was another cause for pity. I can remember the wet eyes of an undergraduate who apparently was overcome by my double misfortune, but I never felt sorry for myself. It was not that I knew no better. Our weekend forays to South Kensington, Buckingham Palace, the British Museum, and elsewhere, had taught me that Shadwell was not typical of London, that there were posher places where people lived better. I can also remember going, as a member of a delegation from the 2nd City of London Sea Scout troop, to wish a merry christmas to a retired admiral who took a very distant interest in us. He lived in a fine row of houses in a square up west—I think it was Thurloe Square, but I am not sure. I was first impressed by the large polished door knob and bell. A uniformed maid left us outside in the street while she went to tell the admiral and through the half-opened door I had my first glimpse of upper-middle class life: white panelling, a dark red carpet, pictures and a polished naval shellcase stuffed with walking sticks and umbrellas. The admiral received us in what I suppose was the library. We stood in front of the roaring fire and were served with biscuits and—of all drinks—dry sherry. As I recall, he did not say much. There was not much to say, and he may well have been embarrassed by our red-cold knees and general raggedness. I did not mind. It was enough to stand near that blazing fire with its brass andirons, sip a rich warming drink in a fine glass, and look at the loveliest room I had ever seen.

I suppose village kids had similar experiences when they called on the squire, or what have you, at Christmas, but they did not have London on their doorstep. We were proud of being Cockneys. I can't remember hearing Bow bells in our house, but we knew that we were Cockneys. We also knew that London was the seat of empire and beyond question the greatest city in the world. We took a vicarious pride in goings-on such as the Opening of Parliament, royal garden parties, Henley and Wimbledon. We never went, of course. I had no idea where Wimbledon was, and thought that Henley was just beyond Battersea bridge, but they were part of London and in a very real sense London belonged to us. I for one was constantly aware of it, the great wen. I used to think that Dickens had called London the great wen. It was only when I read *Rural Rides* that I realized it was Cobbett, but it was always a Dickensian word for me presumably because my London was Dickensian.

The assertion may raise a few eyebrows. I discovered Dickens at a very early age, but the association was not a literary one. I am writing of London of about 40 years ago when it was very much closer to Dickens than that span of years would suggest. For instance, our house was one of the few in the neighbourhood with electricity. The streets were still gaslit and there were regular London particulars. They rolled in from the river, yellowy dirty, and the traffic would come to a standstill or crawl bumpingly along the curb. On Sundays the muffin man still rang his bell carrying his wares in a wooden tray on his head and covered with a worn piece of canvas. We used to wait for him to come and then toast twopennyworth—ten or a dozen muffins—on a long fork before the Sunday fire. Hot-chestnut men still stood on many corners, and at weekends whelks, cockles, winkles, shrimps and jellied eels were sold from stalls with white cloths. The smells and tastes were clean and wonderful. I used to have visions of the sand dunes at Camber—the only dunes I had seen—but they would be blotted out by the naphtha lights and the slyly jovial chatter between the munching and the spitting out of eel bones into the gutter.

Horses and carts were still a common sight, and costermongers' barrows were pulled by donkeys. The main streets down to the docks were paved with stone blocks which were slippery after rain. Watney Street, the main shopping street, was closed to traffic on Saturdays and the stalls lining the pavements were lighted by naphtha flares. There were cries of *Tuppence a pound pears* and *Penny a yard of tape, Ma, wide or narrer* and *Who'd like a lovely toffee-apple*. Spunky apples, or bruised apples, and broken biscuits were sold for a penny a pound. People would sing in the pubs and in the distance you could hear the cry of *Late night final*. It was wonderful when our mother went shopping on Saturday nights. For her it was not real shopping. Owning a coffee shop, she of course bought most food in bulk and at a special rate from a few selected shops. Rather was it an outing. She always wore a coat, unlike most women who wore shawls, and a hat. It was a toque just like the Queen wore, or Mary of Teck as our mother called her. She carried a big shopping bag made of American cloth, but it was never filled. Instead, she would buy a pint of winkles and a bunch of watercress for Sunday tea, perhaps some biscuits and Jaffa oranges, and cake. It was always plain or seedcake, and never jam tarts or Lyons Swiss roll. Nor did she buy from Jack the Banana King, whose stall was at the top of the street near the Commercial Road. We always listened to him for half an hour and more. He would stand on his stall surrounded by stalks of bananas from which he would slice bunches with wildly dramatic swipes of his machete. His voice was hoarse, and he had a wonderful patter. You could see the Carib islands as he described how the fruit had grown warmed by a sun none of us had known. He spoke of the ships in a never-ending stream bringing the fruit to London—and for what purpose? For him almost to give away the bloody stuff to ungrateful so-and-sos. But as far as I can remember he never managed to sell a single banana to our mother. Perhaps she did not regard bananas as real fruit like apples, pears, plums and the occasional Jaffa; or perhaps she regarded him strictly as an entertainer.

When I was a bit older, about eleven or twelve, I used to wander on Sunday afternoons and evenings through the City, up Leadenhall Street with its shipping offices and foreign banks, to the Bank of England and the Mansion House and beyond. One regular stop was a shop at the junction of Queen Victoria Street and Canon Street which sold prints. The attraction was Russell Flint's naked muscular women. I would wander on, to *The Times*, the Victoria Embankment and Westminster. I would gape at Downing Street, stand with reverence before the Cenotaph, and walk across Green Park to Buckingham Palace. I never felt lonely or away from home, but there were parts of London which—I can think of no other word—were cosier than others. Fleet Street, Lincoln's Inn Fields, Covent Garden and Smithfield were special favourites, but I also admired Carlton House Terrace, the clubs in Pall Mall and Bloomsbury.

I never felt an outsider because I only saw London from the outside. Indeed, I felt almost proprietorial. I was benign to Indian students in Bloomsbury and condescending to tourists. I suppose our mother was partly responsible for this attitude, her utter classlessness and her unquestionable belief that she was as good as the Queen. The constant newspaper reading at home must also have helped to create the illusion of belonging, but my London, the exterior London, was a warm and colourful place with its red buses and trams, trees, advertising placards, the lights, the bright Underground stations, and coffee stalls. The warmth was rarely chilled by rain. Instead, the lights were multiplied in the wet streets and puddles and the shops looked more inviting. The feeling of belonging was strengthened when I went to work at the

22

age of fifteen as a messenger for *The Times*. I then belonged to the world's greatest newspaper.

Shadwell was of course the centre of my London, and I must try to describe it without being sentimental or nostalgic. Most of it has gone now, blown to Kingdom Come by Goering's air force. Even the docks have been closed. The church and the New Park are still there, but not our shop or most of the tenements and small cottages. They have been replaced by new blocks of flats, and when I went there on visits from Washington the side streets were crammed with cars and not a shawl was to be seen. I found myself asking if this was what we fought for so many years ago when we kids had sung *Vote, vote, vote for Harry Pollitt* (the communist candidate), *Punch old Janner in the eye* (the Labour candidate), and our parents had voted solidly for Labour. I am not going to venture a judgement. I can say in passing that the welfare state has provided a measure of decent living and opportunity in an area which in New York or Chicago would have been utterly abandoned.

Nevertheless, I walked down the High Street, renamed the Highway, from the site of our mother's shop to the park. It was much shorter than I had remembered, but the park was as trim as ever with flower borders and a well-rolled bowling green. Across the river was the ventilating shaft of the Rotherhithe tunnel, but without its glass dome which had gone with much of East London in the blitz. The park was also changed. The grass was probably greener, and there were placards advertising summer events. No doubt some critic in the *New Statesman* would have claimed that it was now a better organized park, but there were very few people in it. It was in fact almost deserted, and I was sure that the tunnel, which for us was a secret path to the pleasures of Southwark park and its pool, was also deserted except for heavy trucks

23

thundering through. Don't be sentimental, I told myself. What about the poverty and unemployment, and the lining up outside the West Garden gate in hope of four hours' work in the docks?

There was of course no way of checking memory, of separating sentiment from reality if indeed each had a separate identity. But back in Washington, in my air-conditioned office in the National Press Building, I afterwards wrote a column about American ghettos in which I tried to apply some of my own experience of slum life. Whatever new dreadfulnesses were to be found in modern American slums I was certain that the quality of life could be improved if somehow the old East End spirit or outlook could be translated. I don't know if many of my readers understood what I was getting at. For most of them the Shadwell of 40 years ago must have been just as dreadful as modern-day Harlem, but one of them writing from an East End address, understood. Miss Edith Ramsay wrote in part:

'I read your article "Quiet in the Ghettos" last Tuesday in the train from Stepney to Essex where I was going to visit a Wapping boy now teaching in Benfleet. My excitement and delight was almost uncontrollable, and I determined to write and thank you that evening . . .

'I came to Stepney to teach nearly 50 years ago. During the first week I was horrified to be among Jews—I had known no Jews—but after a month I was so in love with the people and the district that I never wanted to leave—and as I retired nine years ago, and I am still here, my wish has been fulfilled. But it is a very different Stepney.

'The area I once knew—as you did—was a district of small cottages, overcrowded, familiar with poverty. We were, as a woman said to me the other day, friends and neighbours. We belonged to Clubs, the children went to Sunday School,

24

if possible to several Sunday Schools to ensure Treats in summer and at Xmas! Mothers were at home and watched and fed their children, for food was cheap. We belonged.

'I think Jewish enthusiasm for education set our standards —and it pleased me more than I can say, when you said our schools were good. Central Schools have gone. . . . Superb new Comprehensive Schools have been built and children have ice-skating, horse-riding, and cruises in the Mediterranean in school time. Juvenile delinquency has increased enormously—in your day, children rarely stole, and indeed there was little to steal. Of course our cottages have been replaced by vast blocks of flats where no animals can be kept and there is no yard or small garden where the father's tools can be kept.

'I welcomed almost every provision of the Welfare State, but our acute and to me insoluble problem is to restore here the spirit we once had.'

Perhaps Miss Ramsay was sentimental. She had a right to be after working and living in the East End for 50 years, but this book does not set out to prove anything. I have been a foreign correspondent of *The Times* for too long. Apart from the laws of libel and obscenity, and those readers who write complainingly to the editor, I am now almost incapable of misrepresenting a perceived situation. Interior bells ring when I stray from the path straightened and narrowed by 187 years of history written according to the standards of *The Times*. The shades of Barnes, Delane and Haley appear when I am tempted, and I meekly return to the old disciplines.

I repeat that I am not trying to prove anything. Rather after a quarter of a century of living and working abroad I have an atavistic longing to re-examine if not re-live my childhood. Of course I must admit to some sentimentality. Over the years, and in the most unlikely places, I have not so much smelled fish and chips as recalled what they meant to honestly hungry people. I have heard the roar and stamp of *Knees Up, Mother Brown* pouring out of a pub on a Friday night. I have felt the sadness of Evensong when we sang *The Day Thou Gavest* and *For Those in Peril on the Sea*. We could see the ships and cranes through the church windows, and some of the other choirboys would look solemn because their fathers sailed regularly to Australia and New Zealand or worked tramps which would not see the London river again for many months.

There are other memories of course. Of friends who might hope for a pennyworth of chips on a Friday night but would rarely have the tuppence to buy a piece of hake or rock salmon. Their parents got drunk on a couple of pints of mild because their constant diet was bread and dripping and stewed tea with condensed milk. Many boys at my school were never really warm during the winter. Some never went to the library. Newspapers and radio were luxuries which their families could not afford. I was aware of much of this. I knew that I was fortunate, but I also knew from a fairly early age that much of this could be changed. The world as reported by the old *News Chronicle* and the B.B.C. was not an unfriendly place, and of course there was the vivid life of the streets, its civility and fortitude. *It's better than being hit on the belly with a wet fish*, was one of the remarks heard in adversity. And there was the river. The fog rolled in, and sirens sounded mournfully as ships dropped down to the sea. I used to lie in bed listening, and dream of when I would be the master of a great ship bound for the Celebes. Why the Celebes, I can't remember. Perhaps it was just too much Conrad. I did not become a seaman, but years afterwards I did get to Makasser and it was all I had dreamed of in that ice-cold East End bedroom. It was soon after the end of the Japanese war, and I stayed with the Dutch administrator. I fished and swam near the old Portuguese fort, and afterwards sat on the verandah in a sarong and sipped cold yellow old Genever. The birds came in with the sinking sun, and there was the smell of curried fish from the kitchen. Music came from the servants' compound, but more often firing from the hills where that year's crop of freedom fighters were busy killing each other.

There were many other journeys. Their enjoyment could not always be traced to that East End bedroom, where I read Maugham, T. E. Lawrence and Hemingway as well as Conrad, but there was often some connection.

Best of all, I can remember returning to England from Singapore by sea after a tour of duty as the south-east Asia correspondent of *The Times*. It was in the early fifties, before I was posted back to India, and we sailed on the *Glen Orchie*. She was a splendid freighter, modern and fast, and had recently been coasting between the Chinese ports. Joe McCarthy ruled Washington in those days, and such trading was very unpopular in the United States. I can remember asking the master why he worked communist ports. He looked at me with almost childish eyes and said, *Because there is trade.*

After three weeks at sea, we anchored early one lovely summer morning off Torbay to take aboard the Channel pilot. All that day and night we sailed along the south coast, past Portland where I had helped to defend Britain with a rifle and five rounds of ammunition after Dunkirk, and Hastings where we had spent our holidays as children. The ship stopped again in the misty early hours, and I went on deck and saw the river pilot come over the side. The ship drove on as if she was still in the Bay of Bengal, but with the siren sounding. As had so many other Englishmen returning from the East, I stood on the deck shivering. I recognized

Greenhithe and Long Reach, where I had sailed a naval whaler as a sea scout. Then came the miles of London docks, and promptly at 8 o'clock in the morning, as advertised months before, the *Glen Orchie* arrived at her berth in one of the royal docks. There was the usual bustle of getting ashore. Patrick, our firstborn, was only a few months old and a Customs officer made a nuisance of himself. I did not have to hear his Home Counties accent to know that he was not a Cockney. Two or three dockers waited while he needlessly went through the luggage, and one of them took Patrick from my wife's tired arms. *Never mind, luv*, he said. *They ain't all like 'im*. He smiled at the baby, and I knew I was home.

# 2

OUR MOTHER'S shop was called *The City of Dublin Dining Rooms*. It stood opposite a street leading to the West Garden Gate of the London Docks where the Irish boats berthed. Hence the name. To the right and next door, on the corner of Dellow Street, was the pub *The Lord Lovat*. Opposite again, but to the right, were the garage and stables of Meredith and Drew, the biscuit makers. To the left, on the other corner of the street leading to the docks, were the West Garden buildings, a gaunt tenement of five floors built on three sides of a courtyard. Each floor was served by a verandah-cum-walkway with iron railings overlooking the yard where children played all day. Their parents would watch from above, leaning over the railings or gossiping with neighbours. A seaman, who lived there, said it reminded him of Naples. I rarely went into the courtyard because non-residents were not encouraged, but it was always lively.

Our shop was double-fronted, with large plate-glass windows bearing two legends in white porcelain lettering. One said A GOOD PULL UP FOR CARMEN, and the other T.G.W.U. UNITED WE STAND DIVIDED WE FALL. The initials of course stood for the Transport General Workers Union to which the dockers and drivers, or carmen, belonged. In each window stood framed slates on which were chalked the daily bills of fare. There were also some potted plants which I was supposed to water. I often forgot, and they looked it. The only entrance was through the shop, and beyond was our sitting-and-dining room and then the kitchen. There was no direct light or ventilation in the sitting room, and the electric light burned all day under a green glass shade. The kitchen was in what had been the backyard which had been roofed over with reinforced glass. It had a large cooking stove, a steamer in which cooked food was kept warm, and a couple of large tables for preparing and dishing out food. A staircase went up one side, first to the lavatory on the landing, and then left to a room where the vegetables were stored and prepared and most of the washing up was done. It was an inefficient arrangement, and dangerous. I was badly scalded when I was about four years old. I was sitting on the stairs playing, and somebody, I think it was Mary, slipped and a big bowl of hot water which she was carrying went all over me. I was in hospital for weeks, and still have the scars on my chest and shoulders. The room at the top of the kitchen stairs and the lavatory were not integral parts of the house, but of a small tallow factory in Dellow Street on the other side of the *Lord Lovat*.

The staircase to our upstairs rooms was in the shop, enclosed in glass and reached through a door. The parlour and two bedrooms were on the first floor, and there was another three bedrooms on the second and top floor. The second bedroom on both floors was also without direct light and ventilation. There was no bathroom, but our mother's bedroom had a washbasin with running cold water. The shop was divided into five stalls, each with a plank table and settles large enough for six people. At the back, against the curtained window of our sitting room, was a table with cakes under glass covers. Apart from the tide table and a religious picture, the walls were covered with union placards and a cinema poster. This was changed every week by the local cinema, *The Paleseum*, which gave our mother two free tickets as payment. There was also a sepia picture of *The Cadby Hall*, a barque on which my maternal grandfather had been purser. A model of a first world war fighter plane hung from the ceiling, and the cage of Polly, our African grey parrot, stood on a chest of drawers against the bulkhead of the stairs. Sawdust was spread on the floor every day.

Ours was a big house by East End standards, and it needed to be. Apart from our mother and my brother and sister, there was our Uncle Lou, Mary O'Brien, Tom and Jim. Uncle Lou, who was father's youngest brother, was blinded in the war when he was 17. He had lived with us since leaving hospital, and paid our mother £1 of his £2.50 weekly disability pension for his keep. Mary was a servant who had come straight from the orphanage before I was born. She was paid fifteen shillings a week and her keep. I did not know the other names of Tom and Jim. Tom had come to London from Lydney in Gloucestershire more years ago than he could probably remember. He helped to prepare the food and did all the washing up, and was paid ten shillings a week and his keep. Jim was an old soldier, and worked as a stablehand at Meredith and Drew across the way. I don't think he was paid anything, but was given lodging and board in return for keeping the shop and the pavement outside clean. He was also the chucker-out, although I don't remember him chucking out anybody.

Tom and Jim ate their meals in the shop, but our house was rather like the compound of a Hindu family. Years afterwards I felt immediately at home when I went to stay with an Indian friend on the Malabar coast. We all lived together, very much together. My sister, Beatie, slept with our mother. Mary had the next room, a glorified closet, which could only be entered from our mother's room.

Uncle Lou and Jim had separate rooms on the top floor, where I shared a bed with my brother, Bill, in the front room. Tom slept in a cot in the corner. The parlour was used only on Sundays and special occasions. Even on Sundays we had to get our mother's permission before entering it. Most of our waking hours at home were spent in the sitting room. It was the only access to and from the kitchen and shop, and much of the day Mary passed to and fro carrying meat and two veg in one direction and piles of dirty plates in the other. This constant activity, and the smells, didn't bother us. Much of the room was taken up by a big table which was the centre of our lives. We sat at it to eat our meals, listen to the radio, read newspapers to Uncle Lou, talk, and do our homework. Most days it was covered with old newspapers, and a big wooden till for the money taken in the shop was at one side. A floral oilcloth covered it in the evenings. Only on Sundays and holidays did our mother spread a tablecloth. Apart from the kitchen chairs, there were a couple of armchairs and a couch. Uncle Lou would sit in a big Windsor chair near the fireplace, reading his Braille books or listening to the radio. It was impossible to take two or more steps in any direction except for the space between the shop and kitchen. Movement in that room was a constant shuffle.

And there was nearly always movement, or intimations of it. When we children were eating our breakfast, Mary would be outside at the back of the shop pouring out great mugs of tea for the customers and spreading bread with margarine and jam or beef dripping. Occasionally a hot breakfast would be ordered, and our mother who was already preparing for the dinner rush would fry eggs and bacon or grill a pair of kippers. The shop would be full when we returned to eat dinner, and Mary would be on the go between the kitchen and shop. Our mother would have little time for us, but we ate well. We ate shop food, except at the weekends, and it was good if heavy. Breakfast was egg and bacon, or sausage and tomatoes, or kipper, smoked haddock, bloater, or grilled herring. There was always fried bread, toast and marmalade and tea. The dinner menus followed an unaltering cycle. I have forgotten the order, but roast beef and Yorkshire pudding was always served on Sundays. During the week came steak and kidney pudding or pie, boiled beef with pease pudding and carrots, Irish stew and mutton chops. We always ate fish on Friday, but never with chips. The afters were mainly steamed pudding of some kind with custard, jam or syrup. Tea was always bread and jam and cake. Supper was cold meat, ham and rat-trap cheese with pickles or a green salad without a dressing. On Sundays we had high tea, which began with meat and salad and finished with tinned fruit and custard. Cakes were also served but the big plate of bread and butter had to be finished first.

With the exception of Tom and Jim, we all ate the two evening meals together, and when we children were not playing outside afterwards sat at the table. Our mother would sit in an armchair knitting, and Mary or one of us would read the evening paper to Uncle Lou from cover to cover, including some stock market prices. I was aware of kaffirs and consols from a very early age. The radio droned in the background while we did our homework or read library books. On Friday evenings we children were bathed in front of the fire in a big galvanized iron tub. Uncle Lou went to the public baths where a good hot bath, towel and soap were available for two old pennies, but I have no idea of when and where the other grown-ups bathed. I think our mother and Mary had stand-ups baths before the wash basin in our mother's bedroom.

The shop was closed for the weekend at noon on Saturday,

33

and for thirty-six hours our communal life expanded and relaxed. Jim scrubbed out the shop which became a play-room for us. Mary would take Uncle Lou up west on Saturday night, to eat in a Lyons Corner House and see a film. He followed the plot quite well with whispered asides from Mary. Sunday was the big day when we could use the parlour. It was airless because our mother kept the window shut to keep out the dust and the street noises, but it was a nice room. It had a piano and a clockwork gramophone, a sofa and two armchairs, and some pieces of furniture which were reminders of her better days when her father was still doing well and our father was a printer on *The Times*. The mantelshelf had many china ornaments and a big clock, and on the opposite wall were tinted photographs of our mother and father taken when they were married. Above the piano was a wonderful picture of the battle of Trafalgar. On Sundays we would wait at the parlour window for the muffin man. We would toast the muffins—they were actually crumpets—in front of the fire, and watch the lamplighter light the street gas lamps with his long pole. It was always a cosy room, especially when it rained and we could hear the ships on the river. I would imagine the captains standing on their bridges regardless of the weather, half-enviously but also grateful for being in that cosy room in front of the fire munching muffins.

Sunday was always a very special day. Nearly everybody went to church, and I for one felt all the better for it. We wore our best clothes and shoes, and were not allowed to play in the street although it was the only day when it was free of heavy traffic. We used to gather again in the parlour after Evensong, and my sister would play the piano. Tom would join us without his apron but still wearing his cap and unbuttoned waistcoat over a clean collarless shirt. He would sit on an upright chair, not saying much but obviously enjoying himself and the room and the fire. It was probably his only enjoyment apart from singing hymns early in the morning. Then he would sing *Abide with Me* even though the sun had hardly risen, but on Sunday nights he would sing *Little Brown Jug*. Our mother and Mary also sang, generally Irish songs such as the *Londonderry Air* and *Down by the Glenside*. The last was a sad revolutionary song about the bold Finian boys. I preferred it to the *Internationale*. It was about a revolution we all knew about, and its sad failure was emotionally very satisfying.

> *They died by the glenside, they died in a strange land,*
> *And wise men have told us their cause was a failure.*
> *But they died for old Ireland, and none died braver.*
> *Glory O, glory O, to the bold Finian men.*

We would all hum the refrain and not look at each other because of the tears. Then we would switch quickly to the *Wearing of the Green*, and stamp our feet happily to the chorus of *They're hanging men and women for the wearing of the Green*.

We were all caught up in the Irish troubles. It is difficult to explain. We were Protestants, and were generally suspicious of our Irish neighbours and Catholicism. Mary was different of course. She was one of us although she went to Mass every morning and never missed a holiday of obligation. She wore the shamrock on St Patrick's Day, but was not a rebel and had little interest in the politics she read every day to Uncle Lou. Few people living in Stepney in those days could have avoided Ireland, but the Protestants might well have been expected to be hostile. They were not, perhaps because of working class solidarity. Ireland for us was what India was for the middle-class intellectuals up west. We knew about Gandhi, his salt march, and the round table conference. We respected him, but had little or no feeling for Indians and other colonial peoples. Ireland was different. It was a class struggle made human by the Irish we knew and the sadness and romance. The Easter Rising meant more to us than the American, French and Russian revolutions. We hated the memory of the black and tans. My idea of a hero was an IRA man in a trenchcoat.

And there were the Irish boats, whose funnels I could see from our front windows. They were also known as the Guinness boats because their main cargo was barrels of Guinness stout. Some of the seamen used the shop, and one of them, a bosun, was a regular. He would sit over a mug of tea until the shop emptied, and our mother could be unusually attentive. I think I discovered why one evening when I opened the top drawer of the chest in the shop. Inside were two pistols, still oiled and in their factory wrappings. They were the first guns I had seen, and I remembered them so vividly that years afterwards when I was commissioned in the army I instantly recognized the Smith and Wesson issued to me. That evening I was fascinated. Our mother a gun runner! I am now certain that she was not, but she must have known about those guns and presumably others. I suppose the shop was what thriller writers call a drop for the IRA, but then I could only gaze at those guns and think of our mother. I don't know how long I stood there, but suddenly the parrot hissed *The tecs, the tecs*. It was one of the few words she knew, but thinking that detectives had arrived I slammed the drawer shut and ran upstairs.

There was not much Irish blood in us. Our paternal grandfather was a French Basque, who had painted scenery for the Drury Lane theatre. He died long before I was born, and I cannot remember seeing a picture of him, or by him. He was supposed to have been a political refugee, which was possible, but probably emigrated only to escape military service. What I do know is that he got off the boat at St Katherine's dock, found a lodging house in Leman Street and settled in the neighbourhood. Our mother claimed he was a great artist. The evidence was a ceiling painting he did in a pub called the *Royal Oak*. Our maternal grandfather was a German named Keller from Frankfurt-am-Main, who for some unexplained reason abandoned his ship in London. He did well, and at one time owned or leased four pubs from St George's to Canning Town. Our mother was born in the *Artichoke*, about 200 yards east from our shop, but she remembered best a pub in Whitechapel which was supposed to be haunted. It was near the theatre and attracted a lot of stage folk. The ghost was said to be that of an actress who was murdered.

Our mother was very proud of her parents. According to his picture, Grandad was a handsome man with a mane of hair and a moustache, and our mother pictured him as another Bismarck. She remembered a few words of German, and liked German food which she would sometimes buy in one of the Jewish shops. She was especially fond of Limburger cheese which she always called Kaese. Our shop was another of Granddad's ventures, and our mother used to say that if he had not lost everything my brother Bill would have finished up in the House of Lords. I don't know why the German failed in his signal duty of elevating my brother to the Lords. Serious business and family gossip were never mentioned in front of the children. But the freehold of the shop was our mother's share of the family inheritance, and she continued to run it when she was married. The reason given was that she was a trained cook. She had worked in some restaurant or canteen run for the staff of the Port of

37

London Authority, but this was hardly a persuasive explanation. Our father was a journeyman rotary printer and his trade, then as now, was very highly paid. He worked at night, until about four in the morning, and could not have seen much of our mother during the week.

There is much I do not know about our mother and father. I have only one memory of him. He was holding me outside a confectioner's shop on the Waste in the Whitechapel Road, and I was eating chocolate. Years afterwards I went back to the Waste and instantly recognized the shop. This isn't much, and I can only suppose that our mother ran the shop because she was a strong-minded woman who liked to be in charge. It was just as well, because we were not left destitute when he died. There was no company pension schemes in those days. Nevertheless, our mother was intensely proud of what she saw as a continuing connection with *The Times*. Her highest ambition was for us to be in the print, but the connection was very tenuous.

At Christmas we were invited to a widows and orphans party in the staff canteen. It was one of the highlights of the holiday, rivalling the pantomime. The high tea was splendid, and we were entertained by clowns and a conjuror. The children were given presents and the mothers £3 for each of their young. The party was organized by Mr Offord, the canteen manager, who always wore the big black bow tie artists were then supposed to wear. In the summer we were invited to the staff outing at Hever castle, the country home of the then Major J. J. Astor, who owned the paper. This was even more magnificent. Special trains took the guests from Victoria to Hever. A chicken and ham lunch with claret cup was served in big marquees by waiters in black coats. Afterwards we could visit the castle and home farm, row on the lake, and listen to a military band. It was altogether a wonderful day. We saw how the toffs lived, and our mother enjoyed herself. It was nice of *The Times* to remember us, but that was our only connection—except the vague promise of a job for us boys when we left school.

Apart from that, our mother was on her own and she brought us up without any outside help. She was 33 when our father died and her life must have been hard in every way, but within limits we all subconsciously recognized we did not want for anything. She was not demonstrably affectionate, I can't remember her kissing me until I marched off to the war, but there was no hardness or bitterness. She talked and laughed a lot when work was done. She was over-protective, as we discovered as we grew older, and we had a strict old-fashioned upbringing. We were taught to believe in God and we did, deeply and unquestioningly. The Sermon on the Mount was accepted as an accurate forecast of our future. We were expected to be clean, and were never really dirty although I was then known in the family as Stinker. We brushed our teeth at least once a day. Thus we were taken good care of in every way with the exception of education.

For our mother, only a minimum of education was required to ensure a good safe job in the print. Bill and Beatie won scholarships to Raines Foundation School, a first class grammar school off the Commercial Road, but they had to leave when jobs were found for them. I am fairly certain that Bill could have won a university scholarship, but when *The Times* beckoned off he went to be a messenger. I failed to win a Raines scholarship, but the church had two in its gift. One was offered to me, but our mother refused and I went to the local central school, St George's. It was a very good school, as were most of the L.C.C. schools, but our mother only dreamed of my working as a messenger at *The Times* and then being apprenticed as a compositor or printer. I think she was very disappointed when I eventually became a reporter.

There was some logic to this. Compositors and printers or machine minders as they were known, were aristocrats of labour. Theirs were highly-skilled and exacting crafts with proud histories. Because of the nature of the job, the getting out of a newspaper every night against demanding deadlines, the men enjoyed a strong craft solidarity. Their unions were also strong. Long before trade unionism reached its present strength, these men had an enviable independence. The Fathers of the Chapel, or shop stewards, were powerful, and the Imperial Father of the Chapel, who represented all the chapels, treated with management in easy equality. The men earned more than ordinary reporters and sub-editors, and their jobs were more secure. Most of them seemed to live in Beckenham or Bromley, mainly because of the all-night train service from Blackfriars but they could afford to live in those middle-class suburbs. Some drove up to Printing House Square in Rileys or Rovers when the average reporter was lucky to run an Austin Seven or Morris Eight. They dressed well, and the older men could have been mistaken for leader writers.

Our mother knew this. She had been married to a printer, if only for a few years. These men were also responsible for raising the money for the widows' and orphans' Christmas parties, and she saw them at the Hever staff outing. The un-skilled or semi-skilled printers' assistants and packers congregated in the beer tents pitched in the castle grounds, but the craft men would play bowls or tennis and inspect the flower gardens. The younger ones danced on the lawn after tea, and always looked superior to the clerks. Some played golf, then a very posh game. No wonder that their well-being, independence and dignity were the limits of her ambition for us. We were working class whatever our grandfathers might have been. It was the Depression, and any comparison with the poor blighters who lined up outside the dock gates for a half-day's work must have been enough to persuade her of the wisdom of her ambition. Apprenticeship papers were passports with which we could move from Shadwell to Bromley.

Strong as our mother was, she was not the only influence on us at home. It could hardly have been otherwise with so many grown-ups in the house, and the most influential after our mother was Uncle Lou. Part of his face was shot away when he was blinded during the last year of the war. Plastic surgery could not have been advanced in those days, but his ravaged face had its own beauty. He must have been very good looking before that shell exploded. The nose, not much damaged, was high and straight. He had a good forehead and wavy hair. His glass eyes could be painful, and he often went without them and wore a bandage. But he always looked alert. His was a mobile face in spite of the bandage, and as he followed a conversation or listened to music I often forgot that he could not see.

He worked at the Admiralty for many years. In the mornings one of us would walk with him to the Underground station, and see him on to the train. He would change trains alone at Aldgate East, and a porter would put him on another to Victoria. He quit after complaining of headaches, but refused to return to hospital or to be admitted to one of the St Dunstan's homes. As with most blind people, he was very fastidious, or particular as our mother used to say. He was always neatly dressed, with his ex-serviceman's badge in his coat lapel. He changed his collar every day, and manicured his nails. He was forever brushing his waistcoat with a handkerchief, and would carefully wipe the rim of his

41

cup before drinking tea. He smoked du Maurier cigarettes which were thought to be very posh.

His interest in the world outside and what went on at home and in our schools were intense. His major influence on me came from the constant newspaper reading. For about two hours a day I read or listened to the news, home and foreign, parliamentary and financial, sports and entertainment—the lot. For much of the time I listened with only one ear as I did my homework, but a great deal percolated into my subconsciousness. Few other children could have been exposed continually to the daily news, and the family interest in politics, which I shared, was thus sustained and strengthened by the daily flow of information. I knew by name most senior members of the British and European governments as other boys knew county cricket players. The endemic problems of Europe were no less well known, and we were convinced that we knew the solutions—collective security, social welfare, nationalization, but never education in the conventional sense.

Because of Uncle Lou, the radio also played a large formative role in our lives. Apart from the news bulletins and the children's hour, we listened to Henry Hall's daily ration of dance music. I can also remember the *Foundations of Music* series. Later I was taken aback by the sneers at Lord Reith's crusade to improve the quality of listening, and of life itself. No sneers were heard in our house. Presumably we had a lot to learn. Quite possibly we were a serious family in spite of the laughter and joking. But certainly it was the rapacious interest of our Uncle Lou that held us silent about the radio set week after week. I can remember doing homework to Bach and Mozart as well as Henry Hall, and the first time I was emotionally overwhelmed by Beethoven's Fifth. I can't say that our mother shared our interest, but she probably thought it was good for us. At least it kept us off the streets, as she used to say. But Uncle Lou's absorption could have prevented her from switching off the set. He would tap his manicured fingers on the table in time with the music until time came to serve supper.

He was also very generous. Our mother used to give us a penny a day pocket money, but every Saturday Uncle Lou gave each of us a sixpenny piece. It was a great deal of money. A Wall's ice cream, bought from a man with a tricycle, cost only a penny. The container part of the tricycle bore the legend *Stop me and buy one*. A bottle of R. White's lemonade or ginger beer also cost a penny. A halfpenny would buy a handful of gobstoppers, tiger nuts, or liquorice in Mr Baron's shop down the High Street. Comics, even innocent ones such as *Tiger Tim*, were not allowed into the house, but I followed the adventures of Harry Wharton, Bob Cherry, and Billy Bunter at Greyfriars in the *Magnet*, which cost tuppence. A packet of five Player's Weights, which we bought from machines and smoked in the school lavatory, also cost tuppence. There was not much else to buy, but our mother insisted that we save half of Uncle Lou's money for Christmas and the summer holidays. The pennies went into brass money boxes shaped like letter boxes. They added up over the year, and with my Sabbath *Goy* earnings I managed to save two or three pounds. This was enough for a Christmas gift such as a Meccano set, or a model sailing boat for the summer holidays.

Mary had no spare money, and no obvious contribution to a growing child except for her amiable Irishness. She was a short woman always dressed in a flowered pinafore except when she went to Mass or Rosary and Benediction or up west with Uncle Lou. She had a red face with nice blue eyes and a constant smile. She was a second mother, and took care of us when our mother was too busy in the shop. She was probably as puritanical as most Irish Catholics of her class, but her amiability was a great boon. She filled many of our emotional needs with much demonstrative affection. Also our mother had little time for Uncle Lou, she was much too busy, and Mary was the only member of the family he could lean on. They were married when we left Shadwell. I don't think our mother liked it much at first, but it was one of those solutions which should have satisfied everybody. Certainly they were very happy for many years in their little flat in Chancery buildings.

Her simple goodness and absolute faith in God were also a great boon. She never mentioned her church to us, perhaps because of our mother. We knew very little about our grandparents, but the origins of our grandfathers suggest that we were once Catholic. I have no idea of when or why our mother became an apostate, but I am reasonably sure that a sense of class, rather than religious conviction, was the reason. The desperately poor in Shadwell, those who got drunk on Friday or Saturday night, were Irish Catholics. Although Mary kept her religion to herself, I think that her goodness helped to explain my return to the church.

Tom was some kind of Nonconformist. He never said, and nobody asked. He came out of the West Country, and an England which had disappeared long before I was born. Shadwell, even in those simple days, must have been utterly alien. He came to us when he went to work as a potman in one of my grandfather's pubs. He was completely dependent upon our mother. He never went anywhere except for an occasional pint in the *Lord Lovat*. At home he prepared endless bowls of vegetables and washed up endless stacks of dirty dishes. He got up soon after dawn and invariably went to bed about supper time, and was always silent in his cot in the corner of our bedroom. In summer Bill and I used to talk while the evening light shone through the light curtains. In winter we kept the light on to read—holding library books above the flannel sheets with mittened hands in that freezing bedroom. Tom never complained.

He was a sweet old man, with a small round face which was always serene. Very occasionally, I would awaken when he got up in the dawn light. He would light a candle rather than switch on the one electric light dangling from the ceiling, and crowd into his clothes. He would take up the candlestick and shuffle down the dark stairs, and soon afterwards would begin to sing hymns. His must have been a dreary life, I suppose, had he not been a member of our family. He also looked after the animals and birds, a dog, a cat, a parrot, a thrush, and the guinea pig I used to keep in the room where he worked. He always cleaned out the cage and spread fresh straw and cabbage leaves.

He went with us when we left Shadwell for Crofton Park in south east London, our first advance towards the promised land of Bromley and Beckenham. I think he was very happy there. We had a small garden, the first I can remember, and he pottered about planting old-fashioned flowers. After all those years he was still very much the countryman. He was very old, and slowly and almost imperceptibly began to fade. First he did not get up at dawn, and then stayed in bed most of the day. The doctor eventually ordered him to Lewisham hospital, where we visited him every Sunday in the public ward. He was much taken by the radio headphones, which he removed very reluctantly when we came. I used to have the feeling that, politely and patiently as ever, he was only waiting until we left in order to return to them and fiddle with the switch which controlled the choice of stations. He actually died while we sat at his bedside one Sunday afternoon, and I have occasionally wondered if we did him a disservice by denying him the radio at the end.

Jim was a very different cup of tea, or rather jug of ale. He was an old regular soldier, whose favourite song was *Old soldiers never die, they simply fade away*. He was an alert man, all of a piece, who dodged about on the balls of his feet as if he was a light-weight boxer. He too always wore a cloth cap, which he seemed to remove only when he was drunk—about twice a week. He then revealed not the short grey hair of Tom but a startlingly shining pate which accentuated his dark bright eyes. When drunk, he would come into the shop and dance little intricate steps. He would sing *The boys of the old brigade*, acting out the lines such as marching shoulder to shoulder, steadily blade by blade.

Like most regular soldiers, he was almost painfully clean. His boots were always boned and polished, as was the old army belt which held up his blue serge trousers. Often I went with him to the Meredith and Drew stables where he was employed as a stablehand. He loved horses, and spent more time than was required currying the great drays. On Friday nights he would comb out their manes and plait them into numerous little pigtails. He would also polish the harness and brasses, and once a year, very drunk but upright, led a team in the horsecart parade in Hyde Park. Jim had served in South Africa as well as the first world war, and had a code of honour which might have surprised his former commanding officers. For instance, he hated Churchill because he was convinced that the late prime minister broke his parole when escaping from the Boers. I must have learned a lot from him, mainly about army comradeship which is not so very different from working class solidarity. As he used to say, you just don't break your word, especially with a first-class soldier such as Johnny Boer.

This was my immediate family. There was a larger family beyond, of uncles, aunts and cousins, but we did not know many of them. One uncle, who had been a carpenter on a British-India boat, was said to have won the Calcutta sweep. He was also said to have owned a fleet of pirate buses before the London Passenger Transport Board was formed. My one meeting with him established that he was wealthy beyond the dreams of Shadwell. He called one day driving up in a Delahaye car. He smoked a cigar, and gave me half a crown before driving away, completely out of our lives, in his enormous tourer. Our closest relatives were the Grooms. Auntie Hettie, our mother's youngest sister, was a little dark-haired woman married to a clerk in the Port of London Authority. In dockland this was affluence and security indeed, but Uncle Jim was always in money trouble. They constantly moved house, apparently to escape creditors. The moving firm which took their sticks of furniture from one part of east London to another was said to boast *We move the Grooms*.

Our poshest relations were the Browns. They were corn chandlers in Canning Town, about four miles east of Shadwell, and Uncle Archie had patented a special mixture of animal feed which had made his fortune. At least it was a fortune to us. They also lived above their shop, but the parlour was twice as big as ours. It had an organ as well as a piano, and Uncle Archie used to play one or the other after Sunday tea. He always wore a smoking jacket and smoked cigars. They were from Holland and had a straw through the centre which was removed before smoking. Auntie Elizabeth, our mother's eldest sister, was said to look like Queen Alexandra, and certainly she was a queenly woman with an enormous bosom. Her dresses were so elaborate compared to our mother's that we knew we were poor relations. This was made evident in many ways. Their children were assumed to be better, handsomer and brighter than us. They also employed a woman as a housekeeper. We did not mind these class differences. They helped to make the monthly visits all the more enjoyable. We went by tram, and our mother would point out the pubs her father had owned. The tea was always splendid, and there were extras such as liquor-filled chocolates and drinks for the grown-ups. Afterwards I would go with my cousin Roland—they all had posh names—to the stables behind the shop and look for rats.

The Browns moved to Wanstead, and eventually emigrated to Canada, but before they sailed we saw them regularly because our father was buried in the City of London cemetery in Wanstead. We went to the cemetery twice a month to tend his grave, to water the little plot and take care of the plants. Afterwards we would go to the Browns or have tea in a bakery. The cemetery visits were outings which began solemnly but changed with the tea. We would walk on Wanstead Flats, an open space which was country for us. Then there would be the long ride home in the tram whose swaying reminded me of a ship. We would sit upstairs, if possible over the driver who stood on an open platform like a sea captain.

Often enough it would be dark when we got off the tram at the top of Watney Street, and we would hurry along past the shops, pubs and tenements to our shop. Our mother would put on a kettle for tea and say, *It's nice to be home*. It was always received as a profound statement with which there could be no possible argument.

# 3

YOUTH is supposed to be a golden age when the sun shines all day long, but I can't remember much sunshine and what is normally associated with it. Visually at least life in Shadwell was very grey, and I suppose this must be one of the main differences between growing up in a slum and in a suburb or the country. Apart from the park and the churchyard there was no greenery. The doors of the by-law cottages opened directly onto the pavement. The aspidistras in the front windows made do for front gardens. Housewives tried to keep back the grime of the streets by scrubbing a half circle of pavement before the front doorway, the bricks of which were whitewashed to waist height. Those who did not were considered very common. The white lace curtains were washed, but in spite of these brave efforts the basic colours of Shadwell were sooty black and mud grey.

Clothing provided little relief except at the weekends. Then teenagers dressed up to go to a dance or the cinema, or just walk up West. They weren't called teenagers. They did not live or pretend to live a separate existence, but for a few years between leaving school and getting married they had a few shillings a week to spend on themselves. Most of it went on cigarettes, cinema and dance tickets, and clothes. Montague Burton sold good suits made-to-measure for 37s. 6d., but the more daring would go to Cecil Gee in the Commercial Road for fully-draped suits, often striped. They wore white shirts and bright striped ties and could look very smart. In winter they wore white silk scarves under their black padded overcoats which were often left unbuttoned to reveal the richness of the scarves and neckties.

The girls still went to dressmakers to have their clothes made. You could see them working at Singer sewing machines at front windows to catch the light. There seemed to be one on every street. Some girls were brightly, even gaudily dressed, and were dismissed by our mother as tarts. Blouses provided the only colour for most, who would wear suits or long coats over their blouses and skirts. They looked over-dressed in summer because light clothing was not generally available and perhaps they could not afford two outfits a year. As the posters said, Friday night was Amami night, and at the weekends their hair was always clean. I can remember our mother shampooing my sister's hair in a basin in the kitchen. The older women who went to church were neatly if soberly dressed on Sundays, but during the remainder of the week they wore their black pinafores and drab plaid shawls. The young never wore their nice clothes then. They were hung up in cupboards or wardrobes until the next weekend while the girls wearing overalls and old coats clattered off in clogs to work at the jam factory in St George's or other factories. The few bright colours were provided by billboards such as the Rickett's Blue placard of a sailing ship and a large white wake. *Out of the Blue comes the whitest wash*, it said.

I may have been especially conscious of the greyness because we lived behind the shop and there was no backyard. The West Garden buildings opposite were four storeys high, the street was narrow, and even from my bedroom at the top of the house not much sky was to be seen unless I stood close to the window. The view opened a bit to the right, but the dock wall was black with grime and topped with a fringe of cranes black in silhouette. Most days one of the Irish boats with a green and black-topped funnel would be in the basin. At high water the bridge and top housing could be seen, and they were almost dazzling in their clean whiteness. At least so it was against the greys and blacks, and when I first went aboard the *Lady Patricia* the rust was a surprise and disappointment.

Then my bedroom was not exactly cheerful. Our mother was houseproud, but bedrooms were strictly for sleeping in. The wallpaper pattern was an intricate floral, mousey with age. It seemed always to be damp and clammy presumably because to my knowledge a fire had never burned in the tiny grate. Apart from the double bed I shared with my brother Bill and Tom's cot in the corner by the door, the only furniture was a wardrobe with a mirror in the door and a washstand on which stood a big china basin and a jug of cold water. The soap, red Lifebuoy, was in an old saucer and our tooth brushes in a jam jar. A chamber pot, or po as we used to call it, was under the bed. It was regularly used. The one lavatory in the house was too far away, down two flights of stairs, through the shop, sitting room and kitchen, and up another flight. The single ceiling lamp was low powered, and no mats covered the dark brown linoleum.

The curtains were thin and did not meet, and the gas street lamp opposite shone in. The green-grey glow never stopped me from sleeping, but caused the occasional nightmare because of the reflection in the wardrobe mirror. I awakened the household one night. I dreamed that I was in the drawing room of a large country house and a full moon silvered the lawn outside. Something or somebody dreadful was in the room. I knew not what, but I had to get out. The french window was locked and I kicked it open just as the something loomed over me. At that moment the light was switched on by our mother, and I was found kicking at the wardrobe mirror with my bare feet. I had never been inside a large country house, and the cause of the nightmare—apart from cheese and pickled onions for supper—remained unexplained. Not so another occasion when I was found on top of the wardrobe shouting, *Heave*. I had been sailing that weekend and the boat overturned and sank.

In spite of these excitements the mornings always seemed to be dark, except in high summer, and the street noises had dark undertones. In winter, when the room was like an ice-box, I used to lie in bed screwing up courage to get up and trying to devise a new procedure for dressing to avoid frostbite. The tried plan offering the least danger was to wear my undershirt under the pyjama jacket and warm the socks and shorts under the blankets. Outside the first horses and carts of the day would move ponderously over the paving stones. They did not clatter so much as grind. I can remember thinking of Sidney Carton in his tumbril and Hemingway's camions moving up to the Italian front. I also used to think of his English nurse and could never forgive him for having to kill her off to finish *A Farewell to Arms*. Afterwards I decided that Katherine was not really very bedworthy, but then I used to yearn for her and the room was that much colder and darker.

Later in the day the High Street, or the Highway as it is now known, was a bustling and lively place. The carmen sitting up on their raised seats would crack their whips, and the harness brasses could jingle. After school I would some-times take a running jump at the high tailboard of a passing cart, and ride towards the Tower in one direction or to the New Park in the other. It was a dangerous sport, and passers-by would shout *Look behind yer, Gov'nor*. The carman would then flick his whip over my head and I would jump off. But not of course in the early mornings.

Another reason for the grimness was enacted outside our shop six days a week, when the casual dock labourers lined up to offer themselves for employment. They would stand in a line on the pavement outside our shop, about 40 or 50 men in ragged clothes and cloth caps with dockers' hooks in their old army belts. Similar groups would line up outside most of the dock gates. The foreman was a big, heavy man, who always wore a bowler hat and in winter a thick, black overcoat. He would walk down the line speaking or nodding to the gangers, and perhaps a couple of dozen men would follow him through the gate for a half-day's work. The others would drift away, a few into our shop if they could afford a cup of tea or Camp coffee, and reassemble at 1 p.m. in hope of being taken on for an afternoon's work. Our mother or Mary also used to watch. They could guess from the number of men taken on how many dinners they would have to serve at midday. But for me, with my head and heart filled with vague plans to make Britain a country fit for the working class to live in, the mornings were further darkened.

Another reason, when I was very young, was school. I shared with most of my mates a dislike of education which our mother did nothing to change. We went to school because we were told that a truant officer would come if we did not. He never came to the shop, and I can't remember ever seeing him, but in my mind he was an ogre no less frightening than Rip Van Winkle, of whom I was terrified. Our mother would only have to say that Rip Van Winkle was coming and I would immediately stop misbehaving or would do what was required to be done. I had no idea who or what he was, only that he had fallen asleep for forty years. Long afterwards I discovered in upstate New York where he was supposed to have lived that he was remembered as a rather nice cosy figure, but for young me he was a very sinister and frightening character. So it was with the truant officer, who I knew would put me in a reformatory school if he came to get me.

In fact, the Highway, and later St George's, were good schools. I was never really unhappy in either of them, and often found some lessons enthralling, but I was badly scarred at an early age at the Highway when I was forced to wear a Little Lord Fauntleroy suit. I have forgotten the occasion when it was bought, I suppose it was a wedding, but once made the purchase had to be amortized. I had to wear the suit until it wore out. In any school or town the wearing of black velvet, pearl buttons and a frilly shirt would have caused the wearer considerable mental anguish, but in Shadwell, London E.1, they amounted almost to a death warrant. I was bullied, scoffed and leered at for what seemed an eternity, but more specifically until one day when I was kicked in the shin by a boy wearing heavy boots. The blow was so brutal that I could not walk for a day or so. Our mother complained to the headmaster, and there was a confrontation in his office. The boy, I think his name was Tommy, was sullen. His mother, wearing a shawl and black pinafore, was very belligerent. It wasn't fair that I should swank about in a fancy suit when she did not have two ha'pennies to rub together or buy food let alone clothes for her Tommy. Our mother retorted that she did not have a man behind her. She was a widow who had to work for a living, and take care of three children and a blind man instead of wasting hard-earned money in the boozers. This did not entirely impress because everybody knew that our mother was not a war widow. This in some odd way apparently made her only a half widow, or entitled her to less sympathy and respect, but I never wore that suit again.

Still our mother had firm ideas on how I should be dressed,

and although they would not have been noticed elsewhere they continued to set me apart from my ragged schoolmates. Until I went to St George's and assumed the protection of a school uniform, I wore grey flannel shirts and shorts topped with a woollen sweater. It was always of a Lovat shade and bought at the Scotch Wool Company. I resented the neatness, and nearly always approached the school warily in the morning.

The Highway School was at the corner of Dellow Street, and the gate less than a minute's reluctant crawl from our shop. It did not fit the usual picture of a slum school. In fact, it was almost identical with the primary schools my children attended in the better part of Washington D.C. some 30 years later. They must have been built at about the same time, just before the first world war. It was certainly more modern than Hampstead Parochial which my youngest daughter went to more than 40 years later. The main building of red and yellow brick with tall windows stood in a large asphalt playground which was divided into two areas, one for infants and the larger for older children. This was big enough to play football and cricket, and the overlooking windows had wire screens as protection against balls which were always being kicked, thrown and bounced. Only the outside lavatories were objectionable by modern standards, and by Shadwell standards the heating was wonderful. I can never forget the warmth of the classrooms on a cold day, or sitting on the pipes in the corridors during the breaks. Perhaps we were lucky, or conditions outside were so drab that the school had attractions not immediately obvious to outsiders. I was also impressed by the solid oak desks, each built for two children, the parquet floors, the many Biblical pictures and the light coming through the tall windows.

Not that we saw it as a beacon of learning or an escape route to bigger and better things. For all the political talk at home, education was never seen to be necessary for progress. We had little or no personal ambition. We never spoke about the future, or really believed that conditions could be improved except by some mysterious political process. The people's representatives would be elected, Hitler and Mussolini confounded, and we would all live happily ever after. For the time being, we just assumed that we would eventually leave school and get jobs, regular ones if we were lucky. The Depression had bitten deeply into our subconsciousness.

We did not of course think of jobs, or much else, in the early years. School was the place where you went to between ten to nine in the morning and four thirty in the afternoon, five days a week. I can remember very little else of the Highway School in school hours, except learning the arithmetical tables by rote and visiting a clinic in Cable Stree. It had been a pub and stood opposite the Flea Pit, the cinema where on Saturday afternoons we saw two films, the news and a serial for one penny. The matinee tickets were red, and when the first performance was over the lights went up and a man shouted *Red tickets outside*. The clinic was visited once every term. Every so often a dentist would inspect our teeth, and eyes would also be examined, but I always connected the clinic with the Flea Pit because at every visit our hair would be inspected for fleas. A nurse in a blue uniform, large starched apron and a black hat with the L.C.C. badge in front, would run a steel comb through our hair. Between each child she would dip the comb in a large enamel bowl filled with some solution and we would claim to see hundreds of fleas swimming for dear life. These were all the health services obviously available at the time, except for free milk given to poor children in school. God knows how authority drew the line because most of us were desperately poor. Perhaps somebody at the clinic decided, but those who went to the little building between the two playgrounds for milk were pitied.

I also have a vague memory of Empire Day, which was celebrated every year. We first congregated in the hall lined up according to our 'houses'. This was a bit of nonsense imported from public and other posh schools. There were no houses as such. The school was just divided into four groups, each with a name and a colour. They were named, appropriately I suppose, after navigators, and mine was Frobisher. The colour was green, and I wore a loop of green stuff diagonally over my chest when playing games for the house. I giggled afterwards, but then we took it seriously enough, and I can remember looking up Frobisher in the public library. Even now, without refreshing my memory, I know that Sir Martin Frobisher sailed from Blackwall—just down the river from Shadwell—looking for the Northwest Passage. And that afterwards he sailed with Drake, after whom another house was named. I was jealous of the boys in Drake because he had been a much more successful navigator. Frobisher had not got very far, while Drake had defeated the Armada and sailed round the world before dying in Nombre Dios Bay. We all knew that his drum would beat should England be in danger again.

Empire Day was rather enjoyed because of this romantic approach to history. I can't remember patriotic speeches, but we did sing *Land of Hope and Glory*. The main event of the day was what amounted to a mass geography lesson in the hall. We squatted on the gritty parquet flooring and one of the teachers pointed out all the red areas on a map. We were told about the self-governing dominions and the promised gift to India of independence within the Commonwealth. The African colonies were hardly mentioned presumably because blacks could never aspire to self-government. The then Malay states, federated and unfederated, were made much of, or perhaps I remember them because of an early addiction to Conrad. Certainly much was made of the British Army standing guard on the North-West Frontier, and of course of the Silent Service maintaining the peace on the high seas. It made no lasting impression on me except— and this is a very large qualification—to establish that I was a freeborn Englishman and the world was my oyster. I developed an expansive and proprietory view of the world which has never quite left me. I am certain that it helps to explain why years afterwards I could fly into India, Palestine, Korea, Singapore, Indo-China and many other exotic and occasionally dangerous places and feel equipped to report and comment on the goings on of the natives. Among foreign correspondents of other countries I have met only the Americans had a similar confidence. In a way it amounted to an awful arrogance, of which I was first made aware by an Israeli in Jerusalem soon after the lifting of the siege in 1948. I had returned from Amman by way of the Mandelbaum Gate, then used only by United Nations people. For an Englishman, still regarded with great suspicion, to cross from an Arab country so soon after the end of the British Mandate was offensive to most Israelis I knew. This one, more perceptive than most, said how he envied the confidence of the British public school man. How different it was for him, a Jew born in Bulgaria. I did not tell him that my confidence, or what-ever it is, was nurtured in a slum school.

It was more than Empire Day of course. Our mother had a great deal to do with it, as did the B.B.C. and the public library but the school did more than celebrate Empire Day every year. We sang songs in the hall two or three times a week, for the most part the usual medley ranging from *Cherry Ripe* to *Jerusalem*. But we also sang *Marching through Georgia* and *Riding down from Bangor* (on an eastern train, after weeks of hunting in the woods of Maine). Years afterwards I realized that these were distinctly American songs, but then the United States was somehow an extension of empire, another pearl in that oyster waiting to be opened. We were also still quite close to the first world war, only six years when I first went to the Highway and twelve when I left. The Germans were very much part of our imagination and fantasy. In most of the non-ball games we played the sides were labelled British and the Germans. It was always German or Jerry, never Hun or Boche. They were always the enemy of course, but respected enemies. The respect they demanded, however, only increased our self-esteem. We had beaten them, hadn't we? As for the French, they were Frogs. I had reservations. After all, one of my grandfathers came from France, but I nevertheless went along with the majority opinion. Summed up, this meant that we, the Brits, were superior people. Not only did we rule hundreds of millions of Indians, Africans, Malays and so on, but we had beaten the Germans—almost in spite of the French. The fact that my other grandfather had come from Germany was a secret source of pride. However you looked at it, we Herens were unbeatable.

Other than that I can only remember the Highway school as a playground. In those days school grounds were emptied and locked after the school day had come to an end although there was no other place in the immediate neighbourhood where we could play, but I was a friend of Reggie Bryant, the second son of the schoolkeeper or janitor. His father was a retired naval chief petty officer stoker. He was a stern and silent man. At least he never spoke when I was in the vicinity. He always wore a navy-blue boiler suit, and his job was to stoke the boilers, superintend the cleaners and generally keep the school buildings in good order. At about 5 p.m. every day he would lock the gates, but because I was a friend of Reggie I could return after tea. The school was then entirely different. The asphalt playgrounds were deserted. Being able to play in an area of about 300 by 200 feet without a mob of kids was sheer heaven. I suppose it was my first experience of space, and at times we would run about like young puppies. We would kick a ball into a goal white-washed on a blank wall, but Reggie was a better footballer and often I preferred to climb drainpipes. I would shin up to the roof of the main building and swing along the gutter; or rather I did until one day I looked down and saw Mr Bryant watching me. He must have been a splendid disciplinarian in the navy because all he had to do was to stand and watch. He did no more, and I shinned down silently and went home with dirty hands and scuffed knees.

Somebody once wrote in *Who's Who* that he was educated during holidays from Eton, and much of my preparatory education was certainly received in the Highway School after school hours and during the weekends. Reggie and I were as close as any two boys could be, and we had this vast area to play in by ourselves. His older brother, Billie, went to a posh school—Merchant Taylors, I think—and spent his weekends playing rugger, which of course was a posh game. In London in those days, and I suppose throughout southern England, ball games were very much part of class differences —for us more obvious than accents. After all, we did not know that we spoke cockney. For us it was the King's English. But the working class played soccer although we did not know it by that name. It was simply football. Then professional soccer players were not the well-paid heroes they have since become. Most of them were nameless except to ardent supporters of their team. They earned £8 a week during the season, which was twice as much as any man in Shadwell could ever hope to earn, but they could not play for ever and only the most fortunate finished up as pub-keepers. Oddly enough, cricket was classless, at least to the extent that we played it during the summer. There was no other game to play. We might have used lamp posts as wickets, but I am sure we were every bit as good as the more fortunate who played with two sets of stumps on some playing field.

But Billie Bryant was superior to us. His family had made the effort to send him to a good school. We were aware of this, and resented it, but not overtly because of our own intensely personal and secret life. This took many turns. In the building used for dispensing milk to poor children we spent hours at the weekend drawing very detailed maps of treasure islands (with X marking the treasure) and of wild west and Crusader forts. We lived out our fantasies. There were no toy revolvers and holsters in those days, at least not in Shadwell, but we made Crusader shields and swords from soapbox wood and cardboard and stormed the steps to the main door of the school to overcome the Saracens. I would bring jam sandwiches from the shop which we would frugally eat as shipwrecked mariners or starving pioneers crossing the Great Divide. Reggie would also occasionally come with me on my walks and rides through London, but not too often because his parents were very strict. I suppose after living in married quarters in naval towns they knew that Shadwell was a slum, and perhaps to be kept at arms' length. As far as I know, they never met our mother, and Reggie rarely came to our shop and I only went inside his house once or twice. But this did not matter because we had the entire school to play in except for the headmaster's room and the carpentry shop which were always locked. On rainy days we would kick a tennis ball about in the big hall or swing on ropes in the hall of the upper school which was fitted out as a gym. Or we would just sit and talk. Reggie and I remained close after I went on to St George's and he to a technical school. He became a toolmaker, and the last time I saw him was in Delhi in the mid-fifties. He was then a manager of a factory in Calcutta.

St George's school was just beyond the Highway between Cable Street and the churchyard of St George-in-the-East, the next parish to Shadwell. It did not front on to Cable Street, and was approached down an alley. It was not as big as the Highway and the playground was small, but it was a very good school. One reason may have been the large number of Jews who attended it. They were so numerous that on Friday lessons ended at 2.30 to give the religious time for a ritual bath before the Sabbath. I think they also explained why German was taught instead of French. With Yiddish they had a flying start. Most of them were children of immigrants who had arrived from eastern Europe before the first world war. Shadwell was well south of Whitechapel, the traditional Jewish neighbourhood, but there were concentrations of them in many streets off the Commercial Road. Lysander Street was the only Jewish street off Shadwell High Street. We knew it as Polish Street because most of the families had come from Poland, but nearly all of my Jewish schoolmates came from the Commercial Road area and its Jewish market. This was an open street market where our mother would occasionally go to buy beigels—bygles in Cockney—and pickled cucumbers—heimischers in Cockney Yiddish—from huge barrels. She would also buy rollmops and soft

62

cheese and what she called Jewish bread, which was rye. This attachment to foreign food, which was explained by our German grandfather, somehow bridged the gap between us and the Jews. *They take care of their own, and know good food*, our mother used to say approvingly.

Because of the Jews, no Christian religious instruction was given at St George's. Or rather Scriptures lessons did not go beyond the Old Testament. This was rather unusual in those days, but what set St George's apart from other schools was that it was coeducational. In each classroom the rows of single desks were alternately occupied by boys and girls. I was told afterwards that it was an experimental school, but not then. It was just the neighbourhood central school which you attended if you lived in the area and had passed the exam. But together with the large concentration of Jews this might well have explained its high standards.

Of course we might just have been lucky in having some good and unusual teachers. I can still remember many of them. Mr Miller, who I think was the assistant headmaster, taught science. It was very general science, and fascinating. He was a member of the Royal Zoological Society, and once a year took us to the Zoo on Sunday, the members' day. I first heard of Darwin's theory of the survival of the fittest from him, and he said with his crooked grin that we must be very fit to survive in Shadwell. I got to know him better when a commercial art course was introduced in my last year. I suppose that because of my tenuous connection with 'the print' lettering or typography interested me deeply. I learned about Caslon, Baskerville, Garamond Bold and Gill Sans, and Mr Miller was impressed by my aptitude. Later at *The Times*, when I had been promoted from messenger to office boy in the Publicity Dept., this training was very useful. It eventually led to my designing the double-crown bills for *The Times Literary Supplement* under the watchful eye of Stanley Morison.

Mr Miller was also a nice man to look at, with a thin brown face, grizzled hair, light blue eyes, and a long bent A. P. Herbert nose. He always wore brown tweed suits with a white shirt and stiff butterfly collar. But not Mr West, the maths teacher. He thought that collars and ties were bourgeois nonsense, and said so in no uncertain Marxist terms. He had to wear a tie in those days of course, but it was bright red because Mr West was, or had been, the communist candidate for some London constituency. The tie was not the only evidence of his politics. About once a week he would cut a lesson short and talk about economics and comment on the Depression and unemployment. I can't remember him talking about communism as such, or party politics, but that was unnecessary. His talks amounted to indictments against the capitalist system, and most of us were willing converts.

Herr Wiener, the German master, was again very different. He was a short, fat man who waddled into the classroom and rested his belly on the desk with a sigh. He wore cropped hair and small gold-rimmed spectacles, and looked and sounded very German. I don't think he liked children. Certainly he could be cruel. One day I was peeling an orange under the desk lid when he waddled in. As usual, we all stood to attention and chorussed, *Guten Tag, meinen Herrschaft*. Instead of the usual gruff reply he suddenly demanded to know who was eating an orange. I was astounded. How could he know when I was sitting in the last row of desks and the orange was out of sight? Too late I learned that oranges had a strong scent and my sense of smell was less than adequate. In spite of his bulk, in no time at all he had seized me by the lobe of the right ear and was dragging me to the front to be ridiculed. I was not one of his favourites perhaps because I was one of the few in the class who did not have the initial advantage of Yiddish. I was therefore a slow starter. In fact, I almost did not catch up because he would send me off to tidy up the stockroom, the chore for dunces. It was a bad start for a future chief correspondent of *The Times* in Germany.

A nicer man was Mr Reece, the music teacher. He was a Welshman, and fanatical about music. We did not sing as much as at the Highway, but instead played and listened to music. He was proud of the school orchestra, which was supposed to have produced some good musicians. I was one of the second violins in my last years at school. The school sold instruments on tick. A violin cost £2, and the weekly repayment was sixpence. Rehearsals were twice a week, and every other Friday afternoon we played in the hall. Again I suppose that the orchestra was better than most of its kind because of the Jews. Some took private lessons, and were regarded as *Wunderkinder* by their parents. Not a few planned to be professional musicians, and one boy played a clarinet in a dance band on Saturday nights. He had a very white face and dark eyes, and it was whispered that he took drugs. On the Fridays when the orchestra was not playing we would congregate in the hall to listen to recorded music. Mr Reece was a Beethoven man, and would talk about the symphony or concerto before it was played. At Christmas time we went to the People's Palace in the Mile End Road to hear Malcolm Sargent conduct.

He stood on a dais with a heavy brass rail on which he would lean when talking to the audience. I remember him as a shortish trim man with dark hair and a lively face who did not talk down to us. His warm voice, the orchestra and choir arrayed behind him, the eager atmosphere and what appeared to me as the richness of the auditorium were wonderfully exciting. I was no stranger to the theatre because of our visits to the Lyceum pantomime and the musical comedies at Dalys and the Coliseum, but they did not prepare me for Malcolm Sargent and the People's Palace. The music was not particularly impressive. On one occasion Sargent asked, *Who is Silvia? What is she?* And I giggled as the choir sang. The stiff archaic language seemed ridiculous. For weeks afterwards I muttered to myself lines such as *That all her swains commend her*, and then giggled again. We heard more exciting music in the school hall on Friday afternoons. I suppose, apart from Sargent, that the People's Palace was exciting because I was hearing live music for the first time.

My favourite teacher was Miss Nixon, who taught English. She was a dumpy woman with no remarkable features. She always wore many ropes of beads and shortish dresses and her flat freckled face was hidden by enormous spectacles. Yet the warm smile shone through even in the classroom. She obviously was in love with her subject and eager to teach. Shakespeare was her special love. This could be a bore because of the set examinations, but we would act out scenes in the classroom. All of us were persuaded to join in mainly by her example. I can remember her bounding into the room as Puck, and she seemed quite capable of putting a girdle about the earth in forty minutes dead. I was a reluctant actor for all her example, and can only remember being congratulated for my impressive performance as Charles the Wrestler in *As You Like It*. Then about once a year, near Christmas, a company would come to give a play in the hall. I don't know if they were professionals or amateurs, but Olivier did not over-impress me when I crossed the water, as our mother always referred to south of the river, for the first time to see Shakespeare at the Old Vic.

Miss Nixon was also devoted to Wordsworth, and again

tended to act out the lines. She would hold out her arms and make wavy motions with her hands when she recited *I wandered lonely as a cloud*. Reported thus she might emerge as a figure of fun, but she was not. At least not for me. She was in love with words, and when she recited Wordsworth's *Composed upon Westminster Bridge September 3, 1802* my Cockney heart swelled with pride. It did again years later when I was home on leave from the army, and sheltering in the Underground during an air raid read a poster quoting it. I still have an occasional twinge when walking along the Embankment towards the Palace of Westminster.

I couldn't spell, and still can't, but that never bothered Miss Nixon much. She wanted us to speak, write and memorize lovely words. I did not like every exercise in writing essays and poems, but I soon discovered that I had a gift of narrative. The occasion was a history exam. I was bad at dates. 1066, 1665, 1666, 1776 and 1787 are the only ones I have firmly grasped, but it did not seem to matter much if I filled up three or four pages of foolscap with colourful detail. Miss Nixon also recognized this gift or knack, and somehow balanced out marks between spelling and essay-writing. This attention was very rewarding. In those days, certainly not in Shadwell, there was no Parent-Teacher's Association or the like. The only time a parent met a teacher was when young Izzy or Jimmy had done something bad. Often a policeman hovered in the background. Social contact was impossible. I don't suppose that teachers earned much, but they were in regular work and did not live in Shadwell. The gulf was unbridgeable even if many teachers were from working or lower-middle class families. They arrived in the morning in their collars and ties or beads and shortish dresses, and disappeared soon after four in the afternoon to perhaps Leytonstone, Brockley or Streatham. Wherever they lived it was beyond our horizon. But the teachers I have mentioned, apart from Herr Wiener, did bridge the gap as far as the students were concerned, and on a personal level with visits to the Zoo and the People's Palace. The treats only happened once a year, but I looked forward to them for weeks and savoured them for long afterwards.

Mr West did not take me to the CP headquarters or to Marx's grave in Highgate, but the almost conspiratorial note of some of his teaching was more intimate and exciting. There were no organized trips in those days for slum kids to Stratford-on-Avon, but Shakespeare, Wordsworth, Keats, Dickens and Jane Austen lived in books and the imagination. Miss Nixon crossed the gap by firing my imagination, and in other ways. For instance, one day after school I was walking back to the public library which was just between the town hall and the entrance to St George's. I had recently discovered Zane Gray, and after reading *Riders of the Purple Sage* in 24 hours flat was going back for more. I bumped into her at the corner of Dellow and Cable Streets, and seeing the library book under my arm she asked me what I had been reading. I had some difficulty in answering because I was still riding through the purple sage. I was chewing non-existent gum, holding in my tummy and the book was really a Winchester 45. I swallowed the non-existent gum, relaxed my tummy and blushed. Miss Nixon did not notice any of this, or pretended not to, and gushed while I showed her the title. She then suggested that we go to the library together.

The Carnegie library was a very special place in Shadwell, second only to the church in its impressiveness. It had a rather grand entrance at the top of some steps, with a terracotta scroll above announcing Mr Carnegie's beneficence. Through the swing doors and to the left was the public reading room. In memory at least it was not so very

68

different from a club reading room. In the middle was a large table with files of all the newspapers, not only *The Times* but the *Financial Times*. Against the windows was a row of desks or tables where people could read. Along one wall were racks for magazines and a shelf of reference books. Men mainly used the reading room, most of them unemployed. At the time this reinforced my high opinion of Shadwell. Even out-of-work dockers wanted to read. Later I knew that most of them came because they had nowhere else to go and the room was warm by institutional standards which were a good deal higher than the temperature at home. Some came to study racing form. One or two old men tried to interfere with children going into the library. It never happened to me, but the first I heard of dirty old men was from schoolmates who had been, or thought they had been molested.

On this particular day Miss Nixon and I went down the broad corridor to the library proper. To the left was the entrance to the children's section and the adults' library was straight on. I returned the book and we went in. It was a handsome room, lined with books of course, and below and above the shelves the walls were darkly panelled. Perhaps only by varnished 5-ply with 2 by 1 inch strips, but for me it could have been genuine Grinling Gibbons. The lights were green-shaded, and there was an atmosphere of calm learning. We went down the left aisle. Had I read Ainsworth? One or two. Dickens? *Tale of Two Cities* the *Old Curiosity Shop* and *David Copperfield* apart from the books we had done in school. Henty? Of course. My one and only school prize had been *At Agincourt*. Percy F. Westerman? Naturally. The *Luck of the Gold Dawn*, the *Good Ship Golden Hope* and the rest. How could you live in Shadwell and not read about the sea? For me Peter Kelso was a live person. This led on to Conrad, H. M. Tomlinson and Masefield. I knew them well. After more of this in polite whispering we went back to the librarians' desk which served the two libraries. Miss Nixon said that I was only thirteen, but one of her prize pupils, and it was time I was promoted to the senior library. An exchange followed, and I thought I knew why. In the senior or adults' library were lots of dirty books which we were not supposed to read. The expurgated *Lady Chatterley's Lover*, *The Well of Loneliness* and the like. Whatever the reason for the exchange, we were ushered through the little gate into once-forbidden territory. At first Miss Nixon was very schoolmarmish explaining the library. Then we went to the end where there were two or three tables and conversation was allowed. We talked about books some more, and she pressed me again about Conrad, Tomlinson and Masefield. Yes, I had read *Lord Jim* and *All Our Yesterdays*, and *Bird of Dawning* was one of my favourite books. I don't know what she decided but we went over to a row of shelves and with her help I selected Darwin's *Voyage of the Beagle* and Hemingway's *Green Hills of Africa*. I did not read Zane Gray again until I was a war correspondent in Korea and he was one of the more literate authors made available by the United States Army. I must say that I had missed something.

My days of course were not given over entirely to listening to music, Shakespeare and the library. After school I played with Reggie Bryant at the Highway or went to church for choir practice or to fool about in the churchyard or the church house. Then there were the Sea Scouts, my rambles through London or playing in the streets. But the divisions were not between school and home. In the shop we listened to the *Foundations of Music* as well as Henry Hall and Harry Roy on the radio. The B.B.C. News and Alistair Cooke were heard in between the variety shows and the Western Brothers. Political talk intermingled with local gossip and family news.

My mother was not interested in education, but we did our homework on the dining table after tea and were allowed to read books undisturbed. Reggie Bryant did not care much for Harry Pollitt or Beethoven, but we both enjoyed the *Magnet* and *Gem*.

St George's nevertheless began for me the separation from Shadwell. It was a slow process if only because the school was not obviously congenial. The vast preponderance of Jewish students prevented me from being absorbed by it entirely. This is not to suggest any juvenile anti-Semitism or anti-Goyism, which seems to be much stronger and lasting than the former. We were just aware of our differences. Families then had strong ties, as did church and presumably the synagogue. Or if not the synagogue the *schule*, or Jewish school most of them attended at the weekends. There was no trouble or unfriendliness at St George's, and outside we were identified by our uniforms. For the boys this was a green blazer with a white St George killing the dragon on the upper left pocket, a cap with the same insignia, flannel shorts and woollen grey socks with green striped tops. Long trousers were compulsory in the fifth and sixth forms although the Jewish boys tended to wear them earlier. The girls wore identical blazers, gym slips and white blouses. The uniforms set us apart but did not exactly elevate us. The best school in the neighbourhood was Raines Foundation where the school tie was remarkably like Eton's. The motto was *Manners Makyth Man*, which I understand Raines shared with Winchester. St George's could not compete. It did not have a motto, and was rotten at games, but in a curious way we were different. There was the Jewishness in which I took some obscure pride, and the mixed classes. I can't remember much obvious mixing of boys and girls but somehow it did rub off some rough edges.

71

To this day, after investing a great deal of money in the education of my four children, I do not know what makes a good school. Obviously if I had stayed at the Highway it would have been different. It was very plebeian. Of course I was younger, but the older boys who stayed on seemed to glory in what I suppose must be described as working-class attitudes. I retained my share, and enjoyed them fully. I am still rather proud of the few which have persisted. But the basic attitude, of being proud of being at the bottom of the heap which can nourish class solidarity but is individually stifling, I lost at St George's. The teachers may have been motivated by Victorian uplift, but in a very real and exciting way they did lift me up. I suppose they are now very old or dead, but I salute my memories of Mr Miller, Mr West, Mr Reece and, above all, Miss Nixon. This may sound disloyal to Shadwell, but is nothing of the sort. They were as much part of it as the dock walls and the ships' sirens sounding in the night. Without their help those sounds might have been only disturbing.

*4*

EVERY SUMMER our mother took us to the seaside for two weeks. As a child she was often taken to Yarmouth, and thereafter frequently spoke of Norfolk as if it was the south of France and of Yarmouth as a superior Cannes. No sand was more golden or extensive, no front grander than Yarmouth's. *My old dad*, she used to say, *would have nothing but the best*. We accepted this as gospel, no matter how often it was said or in whatever connection. But we always went to Hastings which had a shingle beach, and the little sand it had was exposed only briefly at low tide. We never asked why we did not go to Yarmouth or any other resort. We never questioned our mother once her mind was made up. She had a way of talking to Mary over our heads. The impression was of our participating in a family discussion, but we were only present. And Mary would agree to everything our mother said.

This applied to so-called discussions on every subject, but I remember the holidays particularly because they were so important and because we began to talk and think about them soon after Easter. The talk followed a fixed pattern. After the obligatory reference to the glories of Yarmouth, our mother would review the pretended alternatives. She would begin with Southend, which was quickly dismissed as too common. Whelks and cockles and Guinness on the beach if you could find it when the tide was up. And when it was out there was nothing but mud. Margate was not much better, although she changed her tune afterwards when she retired to nearby Birchington. Broadstairs was not for the likes of us, although we did go there once for the day on a charabanc. I remembered it as a quiet little place with a hotel on the cliff where Dickens wrote one of his books. A house on the headland was supposed to be Bleak House. Broadstairs has since changed, but then after that excursion I assumed that it was a bit too posh, a place for children who could go to school in neat clothes without comment. I can also remember a girl on the beach who was friendly at first but then drifted away. I suppose it was my accent.

Brighton was vulgar, fit only for illicit weekends. Our mother never used these words, but the oblique remarks to Mary were enough. We too read the newspapers, and knew about detectives entering hotel bedrooms for evidence. She would progress along the south coast until she reached Bournemouth, which obviously appealed to her. *Just like the tropics*, she used to say. *What with all those palm trees*. The impression left was that we would go there one of these years, but not yet. Always we returned to Hastings, which was just our kind of place apparently. *Nice and reserved*, she used to say. *People keep themselves to themselves, but are always ready for a good laugh*. The readiness to laugh was highly valued.

For all the inevitability of going back to Hastings, she was supposed to be open to suggestions until about May when she wrote to Mrs Wilkins who kept the boarding house in Bourne Street where we always stayed. Until then I would extend my walks through London to the main line stations to watch the trains and crowds and look at the travel posters. They were standardized in design, with a large colour picture almost invariably of a clean sandy beach, blue sky and a white-capped but friendly sea. On the horizon were sailing boats and sea gulls, and to the side a suggestion of municipal gardens, hotels with striped awnings, an old castle or a harbour. Above would be a legend such as *Come to Bracing Skegness*. I liked best Liverpool Street station which had a footbridge over the platforms, and I would watch the trains coming and going regularly enveloped in clouds of steam and smoke. But Liverpool Street was the station for Yarmouth, and I would then walk or ride a cart or lorry to the old Southern Railway stations, London Bridge, Cannon Street, Charing Cross, Waterloo or Victoria. The boat trains for France left from Victoria, and sometimes on a Saturday night I would stand by the gate for the Golden Arrow train and watch the taxis arrive with what appeared to be exciting people. Charing Cross had a special place because I knew we left from there for Hastings. London Bridge was very special because of the hopping trains.

I only went hopping once, but most of my chums from the Highway school went every year. I used to envy them because hopping was for East Londoners a folk custom, a fixed part of Cockney life. We never went as a family because our mother had enough money to take us to Hastings, and she liked to keep herself to herself. For most of my chums hopping was the only holiday they could expect. Hopping of course was hop-picking. The big breweries and independent growers needed a lot of labour in September to strip the vines. There was not enough locally and over the years a mutually beneficial arrangement developed between the hop fields of Kent and the East End. Whole families would go down for two or three weeks, to pick hops by day and drink in the local pubs at night. They were housed in long huts, one room to a family, and not much better than cow sheds. Today I suppose the health authorities would not permit such living conditions, but then nobody cared and the hoppers enjoyed themselves and made a little money.

Most went by train, and specials were run from London Bridge late at night. The scenes were extraordinary, fit for a Hogarth. The hoppers had to take bedding and cooking utensils, and of course they could not afford luggage. There were bundles or sacks of bedding and clothes, and pails or old boxes stuffed with frying pans and pots. The men, already a little tipsy, wore their work clothes, and the women, struggling with children and bundles, the usual black pinafores, shawls and caps. The trains were old, and the long passages leading down to the platforms were dingy and dimly lit with gas flares. The fare was cheap, but costly enough for an unemployed or under-employed man with a family. Local myth had it that some mothers hid children under their pinafores to avoid paying for them, and that the ticket-collectors were armed with long hatpins. These were supposed to be passed through the pinafores, the assumption being that the screams of young illegal travellers would reveal their presence. Myth also had it that youngsters had been blinded in the process, but none of my mates was one-eyed.

The only time I went hopping, I travelled by lorry which was cheaper than the train. I went with the family of a boy who belonged to my Sea Scout troop. About four or five families went, and by the time we all got aboard we were stuffed like sardines. It was an old lorry, with a canvas roof and high tailboard against which most of the youngsters sat with a mother to keep an eye on us. It was a wonderful trip, the first time I had been away from home alone and the first time I legitimately rode on a lorry. I was about thirteen. The journey was no more than 30 miles, but it took about two hours including one stop at a pub and it was after dark when we reached the hopfields. The driver lost his way somewhere between Tonbridge and Wateringbury, and we stopped at another pub to enquire—and of course for the grown-ups to have another round of drinks. There was a fish-and-chip shop nearby and we all had two-and-a-pen'orth, or a tuppenny piece of fish and a pennyworth of chips. It was lovely, especially for me because our mother despised fish and chips as much as shop cake. I was in fact twice blessed.

When we at last got to the hopfield it was a saturnalia of flickering hurricane lamps, staggering figures with long shadows and drunken singing. The several lurching groups were singing different songs, but the most popular was *Nelly Dean*.

> 'There's an old mill by the stream, Nelly Dean
> Where he used to sit and dream, sweet Nelly Dean.
> And the waters as they flowed seemed to murmur soft
>     and low,
> You're my heart's delight, I love you, Nelly Dean—
> Sweet Nelly Dean.'

The harmonizing went on and on until a persistent beat triumphed, and everybody was singing and dancing *Mother Brown*.

> 'Knees up, Mother Brown. Knees up, Mother Brown.
> Under the table you must go, eeh-eye-eeh-eye-eeh-eye-
>     oh.
> If I catch you bending, I'll saw your leg right off.
> Don't get the breeze up, just get the knees up,
> Knees up, Mother Brown.'

I had heard all this many times before from the crowds outside the *Lord Lovat* next door in Shadwell, but it was very different after a long lorry journey and in a strange field near the Medway river. I was scared. Perhaps the long shadows made the dancing seem more abandoned than it was.

But my surrogate mother shepherded me and her own flock into the room which her husband had established was ours. I took little notice of it that night. All I can remember was that I was given a straw-filled palliasse to share with my chum under an army blanket. I had a dreamless sleep until dawn. I awoke early because I was cold, and the early sun was shining through the cracks round the door and the shuttered but glassless window. Tommy, my chum, had the blanket tightly round him. It would have been impossible to have unwound it. I put my shoes on and went outside. It ought to have looked tawdry after the night before, but in those not so distant days men did not make so much litter. The grass was trodden, and beer bottles sparkled with dew, but it was still a lovely morning like nothing I had seen before. I was aware of the hopfields on both sides and behind, and oast-houses rising above the vines, but the ground sloped away in front into a thick mist. I walked down hill into the mist, across a pasture and a road and then into a riverside meadow.

I had recently read *The Wind in the Willows* and had shied away from the embarrassing chapter in which the author communed with nature. I did not reverse my judgement when confronted for the first time with a small country river, but it was nothing like the Thames at Shadwell. It was like a green dream. The meadow dropped down to a reedy bank and on the other side were willows, which I recognized, and beyond a line of tall trees which afterwards I learned were elms. Between the reeds and willows the river was about thirty feet wide and downstream, to my left, was an old stone bridge with three small arches. Overall was a mist thinning as the sun rose above the trees and a wonderful stillness. My shoes and socks were wet from the dew, but I sat on a tree stump, searched for a battered packet of five Players Weights in my trouser pocket, lighted the one remaining crumpled cigarette and waited for Rat to appear. I thought I saw him, a small nose marked by a slight wake under the willows opposite but he was quickly gone. I finished the fag, almost burning my fingers because the dog-end was so short, and sauntered along the river until I reached a small village up on the road. It was still early but a general shop was open to sell the Sunday papers, and I bought the *News of the World* (which we never had at home), another packet of five Weights and a penny bar of chocolate. I then sat at the foot of a small war memorial, ate the chocolate and looked at the weekend news with my second cigarette of the day.

I can remember this very clearly because it was such a lovely morning and my first away from home. It was also the first time I had breakfasted off a chocolate bar, and for all my bravado the first time I had smoked outside the school lavatories. Also for all my Cockney gregariousness, my friendly recognition of people who came to collect their Sunday papers, nobody returned my salutations. I supposed that they did not want anything to do with hoppers, which annoyed me. I wasn't a hopper. Our mother took us to the seaside every summer, but the experience reinforced the impression that we Cockneys were a race apart. Eventually a policeman came along on a bicycle and asked which hop-field I came from. I did not know of course, but pointed down the road. Not too unfriendlily, he said that I should get back to where I came from. As an afterthought, perhaps because he thought that he had been too brusque, he said that my mother would be worrying, but I went on repeating in my mind a refrain I had grown up with. *If you know a good copper, kill him before he goes bad*. When I got back the women were cooking over a variety of fires. My surrogate mother was annoyed because of my unannounced absence but relieved to see me back. I had a second breakfast of bacon and fried bread and a big enamel mug of sweet tea.

I spent only a week in the hopfields, but enjoyed it immensely. The weather was splendid, if cold at night, and the work was not hard. No skill or muscle was required to strip the vines, and the little family groups working between the poles were fairly friendly. The only squabbling was with the man who weighed the sacks of hops—the pay was according to weight—and there were lurid threats of what they would do with him after the last bag of the holiday had been weighed. The favourite plan was to stuff him in the fire of one of the oasthouses where the hops were dried. One comic wondered if it would affect the taste of the beer. Another told a tall tale of how the year before at another hopfield near Paddock Wood they had chased the weighman down to the river and tossed him in. Similar tales and threats followed. A particularly unpopular police sergeant at the King David's Lane station in Shadwell had recently been transferred, but it was claimed that he had been put in an empty Guinness barrel and shipped to the brewery in Dublin. This was typical of one variety of Cockney humour, of the sense of being surrounded by a hostile or uncomprehending world but sticking together, having a good laugh, and triumphing in our own fashion. For me, the week seemed to be one long picnic. Only breakfast was cooked. For lunch we had bottled cold tea and bread and cheese. Tea was bread and margarine and jam or bloater paste with freshly brewed tea, and we had fish and chips or just chips in the evening from the shop near the pub in the village. Most of the grown-ups spent the evenings in that pub, except on Saturday night when they crossed the river to drink in another which closed a half hour later. We used to hang around, kicking a ball on the small green and drinking R. White's ginger beer or lemonade.

Occasionally we swam in the river but it was September and the water was cold even after the hot afternoon sun. We also tried fishing with a rod cut from a willow, but somebody complained and the next evening a policeman stood warningly on the bridge. The older boys chased girls, but we were too young. We would go back to the hut alone, and be asleep when the grown-ups stumbled in, but I awoke at least once. They were very amorous that night, but I could not see anything.

That hopping holiday helped to explain why our mother always went to Hastings for the summer fortnight. Hopping was not only a folk custom, but a temporary extension of London's East End into the countryside. There was no escape from it. The hoppers were herded into sheds, and only a few pubs would take their money. The others had signs in the windows saying that hoppers and gypsies would not be served. They were probably illegal, but nobody wanted to go where he was not wanted. Few hoppers went beyond the nearest pub and general shop. The children wandered a bit, but not too far. They were soon made aware that they were not wanted, and in any case did not know how to amuse themselves in the country. Our mother did not know this, but she did know that she wanted—or was driven by some inexplicable force—to escape from Shadwell even though she was one of its ardent defenders. She was a powerful woman, strong minded, and for all the inhibitions of relative poverty and conventional thinking in what was still a deferential society, a very determined and free-minded woman. She would have made a splendid pioneer mother. She was also a handsome woman. Widowed at the age of 33, I had no idea how she suffered, as she must have done. She had the wonderful Cockney gift of accepting a situation, and making the best of it, but for her the Hastings holiday was much more important and exciting than for us. For 50 weeks of the year she ran the shop and took care of us, but for two weeks she was determined to be free of Shadwell, if not of us. If we went to Hastings every year she could still see new faces and talk to people outside Shadwell. This immediately became evident on the train down to Hastings.

It was quite an expedition although the distance travelled was less than 70 miles. There were the four of us, with two big suitcases, a paper carrier bag for the sandwiches and two model sailing boats. My brother had a beauty, a schooner with a green and white hull and a little varnished deckhouse. I had a ketch painted red. It would have been easier to have carried them dismasted, but we always rigged them before setting out. A taxi to Charing Cross station would not have cost much more but we travelled by Underground. This meant struggling down and up staircases, and changing at Aldgate East. And we always arrived too early.

When the train eventually backed into the station we would seek out an empty third-class compartment, but it would quickly fill. Our mother would then behave in the accommodating Cockney manner, moving us along the benchseat to make room for others even though it meant some discomfort for her and for us. Then keeping herself to herself (her favourite remark), she would watch for an opportunity to talk, to reach out beyond Shadwell and her widowhood. She would have an averted, even sly gaze, but as we moved up reluctantly she would say something obvious about the weather or the train and then launch into conversation about the attractions of Hastings and whatever was the news of the day. She was always tentative. If the addressed was silent, or disagreed or referred to something else, she would begin again. Once launched, she would put on what we called her posh voice. The aspirates would occasionally be misplaced, and must have sounded awful, but she and we were blessedly unaware of that.

The important thing for her was that she had broken through a barrier. She was reaching beyond Shadwell and the shop with its kitchen, living room and lonely bedroom. Beatie, the oldest, would show embarrassment, and perhaps was ashamed. After all, when I was twelve she was seventeen. About halfway, the train always stopped at Tonbridge or Tunbridge Wells when it was time for us to eat the sandwiches. Food was important for our mother. She could make deprecating remarks about her cooking, but for her even eating a sandwich was a sacrificial act. A great fuss would be made over opening the packets wrapped in newspaper, and after seeing that we were fed would offer the remainder to the other passengers. I can see her now, eager to talk, ready to retreat, but more than half convinced that the human race as represented in the compartment was as friendly as she. The hand proferring the sandwiches, with the little finger half bent, had its work-hardened beauty accentuated by the thin half-moons of dirt under the nails. Perhaps this was why they were more often than not refused, but she would talk on until we reached Hastings. She would then wish everybody goodbye as if she had known them for years.

We would stagger down the platform with our luggage, and our mother would hand up to the engine driver the *News Chronicle* she had brought from the shop. I assumed this was part of the ritual of travel, and was proud of our mother for being fully informed on such matters. It was also an opportunity to get near to the engine driver, and say hallo. In those days they were highly regarded by boys because engines were more exciting than jet planes and even spacecraft are for my children. The special place occupied by the engine driver was also acknowledged by many grown-ups who would nod or say something as they walked by. The driver, wearing a narrow stiff collar and black tie, would look down from the footplate expecting the acknowledgements and greetings. Billie and I were primarily interested in the locomotive. We knew every type with its combination of axles. The engines on the Hastings run were quite ordinary, but after reading about engines, and collecting cigarette cards, they were at least real. We had travelled by rail. And as ordinary as they were, the green paint was oiled and the brass and copper polished.

Then we would go through the ticket hall into the station yard, and it was like going into another world. We could not see the sea, but everything was cleaner and brighter than Shadwell. The change was tangible. Passers-by were sun-tanned, the women wore cotton dresses, the collars of the men were open and the children bare-legged. We would get on a trolley bus which travelled parallel to the sea, but we never saw it until just before the fish market. Then the sky suddenly opened, and the horizon fell back for miles, and it was like embarking upon a long sea voyage in spite of the constant hiss of the trolley bus. By this time our mother would be getting the bags together, and looking forward to a nice cup of tea which Mrs Wilkins always had ready.

The boarding house was just round the corner from the market. It was one of a terrace of houses, narrow and three-storeys high, and painted a tan colour. We always had the two rooms on the top floor, from which a tiny piece of sea could be glimpsed between some houses. There was no bathroom, and the lavatory was in the backyard. We had breakfast and high tea in the kitchen, served directly from the oven in the fireplace. The kitchen was very cosy, lighted by a gas lamp coming out of the wall near the fireplace. Mrs Wilkins was a kindly woman, who always wore a clean white apron. She made a fuss of us, but we were not invited to linger. It was the only living room in the house, and others had to be served. The food was good, especially the high tea. There was always fish, because Mr Wilkins was a fisherman, and Cockney delicacies such as winkles and whelks and cockles. The kippers were marvellous. Another treat was early morning tea which was left on the little landing outside the bedrooms about half past seven. For all this our mother paid only £3.3s.od. a week plus the cost of the food.

In those days Hastings was a pleasant seaside town. The better part was near the pier where the promenade was lined with hotels and superior boarding houses known as guest houses. Opposite the pier was the Winter Garden. I did not know what it was. We never went inside. There were obviously invisible lines which our mother never crossed, but we vicariously enjoyed the suggestion of comfortable middle-class living. The promenade was new, or had recently been rebuilt, and had well-tended gardens. There were then very few motor cars, and the front was uncluttered, clean and expansive. Strolling was a simple joy, especially in the early evening when we would peep into the hotel dining rooms and lounges admiringly and without envy. We even enjoyed the rain because unlike in Shadwell it made the town cleaner. Everything, roofs, windows and pavement, shone after rain.

We rarely went beyond the pier. Beyond was St Leonards-on-Sea which was too quiet and posh for us. Eastwards the promenade continued down to the Old Town and the fish market apparently unchanging, but the number of small shops gradually increased and the houses became older, smaller and plainer. As with many seaside towns, Hastings was originally built in a gap in the cliffs, and behind the older section of the front was the jumble of narrow streets of the Old Town. Parallel to the front was East Street, a narrow, bustling shopping street with old-fashioned family grocers, butchers' shops and newsagents with bawdy postcards in the window and stacks of buckets and spades in the doorway. Halfway down the street some steps led to a smugglers' cave, and at the end was Reeves where we always had dinner at midday. It was like our shop in Shadwell, but was much bigger with long tables at which could sit perhaps a hundred people. The food was also similar. No matter the weather, hot or cold, every day I had roast beef, Yorkshire pudding, roast potatoes and runner beans. It cost 9d. Steamed pudding with jam, syrup or custard was 2d., and a mug of tea 1d. Thus I had a good blowout for a shilling or the equivalent of 5p.

All Saints Street began at the fish market and joined the London road. For us it was a bit of Olde Englande, although trolley buses hissed up and down all day long. The houses were old and generally run-down, and the overall impression was pre-Georgian. Sir Cloudesley Shovel had lived in one of them. I knew nothing about the 17th-century admiral, but I always admired the low slanting house with its crooked door. At the top of the street opposite the church was a sloping meadow where we used to sit some afternoons and watch the traffic on the London road. The grass was luxuriously thick and decorated with buttercups and daisies. I used to lie on my back with my eyes closed against the sky. listening to the buzz of flies over the cowdung and dreaming of Puck. Not Shakespeare's, but Kipling's Puck. I had read and re-read *Puck of Pook's Hill* and *Rewards and Fairies*, and more than half believed that he and Saxon lords and Norman knights still haunted Sussex.

The East Hill was Puck country. It was downland sweeping up two or three hundred feet from the Old Town, and dominated by the remains of a Norman castle. Beyond was what appeared to be limitless grassland, occasionally streaked with chalky ruts and broken by gorse, marching along the sea to Fairlight Glen. For us, the glen was the most beautiful place in all England, and superior to the Bay of Naples. So our mother had told us, and we willingly believed her. We were already developing her reassuring proprietorial approach to places and things. It was indeed a pleasant fold in the cliff although we rarely ventured too far down it because it was too steep for our mother. A bus or trolley went as far as the head of the glen, but this municipal convenience did not detract from its beauty or suggest that the downland was not limitless.

The West Hill immediately behind the town was much built upon, but it had a stretch of grass not unlike a common and surrounded by red-brick houses with painted gables. It must have been a pleasant place to live even with holiday-makers dotting the grass, and was utterly different from the part of the town under the East Hill. Here the promenade became a narrow road and ended at Rockanore. When the wind was blowing the waves would break over the railing, and I would stand there in my school blue macintosh with narrowed eyes and as brave as a destroyer captain on the Dover Patrol. The road to Rockanore was lined with fisher-men's cottages perched precariously under the cliff. On the beach side were rows of tall tarred huts in which the fisher-men kept their nets. Then came the lifeboat house and a small chapel known as the fishermen's church. A broken harbour wall stretched out to sea, but it served only as a breakwater. The fishing boats were winched up on to the beach. They were about forty feet overall and heavily tarred. They were power-driven, but carried jib and mizzen sails which were hoisted when the fishing grounds were reached. Most of the boats had a small wheelhouse.

The fishermen wore navy-blue jerseys and little peaked caps, and some a gold earring in the right ear. They did not appear to do much fishing, perhaps because they often fished at night. During the day they would dry and mend nets and stand outside the pubs. They knew that they were one of the town's attractions, and willingly played the part. Grown-ups were permitted to buy them pints of beer, and we children to push at the winch bars. Judging from the giggling at night, the girls were also permitted to make their offerings.

We enjoyed the many attractions of Hastings fully, but by seeing, doing, feeling and dreaming rather than consuming. With our penny-a-day pocket money we would buy an ice cream cornet, a Wall's *Snofrute* or an R. White's drink, but apart from food our mother did not buy much. We never saw a show on the pier or at the Winter Garden, or hired a deck chair. We only went to the cinema if the weather was really atrocious. Our enjoyment was rather formalized. The fortnight always followed a fixed pattern. The beach and sea were the prime attractions, of course. We were out of the boarding house by nine in the morning and went straight to the beach except on Sundays when breakfast was later and we went to church afterwards. If rain came we sat in a shelter on the promenade. When the tide was out we would dig sand castles, paddle in the sea, or play cricket with one bat and shoes to mark the wicket. When it was in we would sit on the shingle or swim. We never spent tuppence to undress in the canvas booths lining the wall of the promenade. Even Beatie was expected to get in and out of her swimsuit, then known as a bathing costume, under a towel or macintosh.

I can dimly remember using a bathing machine when I was very young. These resembled old horse caravans, and were designed in Victorian times to permit young ladies to bathe without offending their modesty. They undressed inside the machine which was pushed into the surf and beyond the vulgar gaze of those on the beach. They had the extra advantage of conveying the bather into the water. Instead of the double discomfort of stumbling over shingle barefoot into the sea, which could be excruciatingly cold as it lapped over the ankles, the fortunate user of a bathing machine walked down some wooden steps right into the sea. I can't remember how I got into such a machine. Our mother would never have wasted money on such devices, and in any case they had disappeared by the time I was eleven or twelve.

We never spent long in the water. Although it was the main attraction, you could not do much once you were in. Swimming was difficult because of the waves or swell, and the undertow of receding water frightened me. We had all been primed with horror stories about the strongest swimmers being swept away and last seen disappearing towards France. It was also cold. After some minutes of trying to swim, and splashing with much bravado, our teeth would begin to chatter and our skin turn blue and we would not resist for too long our mother's call to come back and dress. We would dry ourselves on the one towel our mother allowed us, and spend the rest of the morning paddling and enjoying the scene.

There was much to watch. Every day a paddle steamer would leave the pier for one of the French resorts. Speedboats took holidaymakers for short trips along the beach at half-a-crown a time. We never went in the speedboat or on a one-day excursion to France. When our mother did not want us to do something, generally but not always because of the expense, she had a trick of eradicating the possibility from our minds. I don't recall how she did it. I wish I did; it would be useful with my own children. I suppose we must have co-operated in the self-deception, but somehow it would be agreed that the forbidden project was not for the likes of us, or at least not this time. But the speedboat was hard to reject. I would watch it roaring back and forth along the beach, or in the evening would stand at the end of the pier and watch the lucky ones climb down steps to board it. The driver or pilot was a big strapping chap, who wore a sweater and swimming trunks. He was burnt dark brown by the sun, and his yellow hair and moustache were bleached. He looked friendly, and might have given me a ride for half price; or so I thought, but 1s. 3d. was the equivalent of fifteen ice creams or more than two weeks' pocket money.

Occasionally a big ship could be seen on the horizon, a freighter or P & O from the London river, or so we told each other knowingly. Our mother, who was the acknowledged expert because of her cooking days with the Port of London Authority, would say it was from Tilbury or one of the royal docks. This could be almost as good as taking that one-day excursion to France, although not going on the speedboat. The only boats we got on were the launches the fishermen ran from the beach. They were about thirty feet long, and carried about sixty passengers. For a tanner, or sixpence, you could go beyond the pier in one direction and the harbour wall in the other, a trip lasting about half an hour. The boat never left until it was crammed full, but we didn't mind. We only had one trip each holiday, and sitting aboard, rocking gently in the swell, and looking disdainfully at other kids on the beach was half the fun. We giggled at the old mums struggling aboard. The fishermen had little portable landing stages against which the boats would ride, but it was not easy for a sixty-year-old in long skirts, clutching her bag, often a shopping bag as well, and her hat against the wind, to embark. There would be good-natured banter, and much tugging and pulling, then bursts of laughter and shouts of Oops as stout old party collapsed into the arms of the waiting fisherman.

The best days to go on a boat-ride were Wednesday or Saturday when beanos were held. They were also held on Sunday, but we were not allowed on the beach. A beano was an annual excursion organized by a firm or club. The organizer would collect a few pennies a week throughout the year, and the total was sufficient to hire a motor coach for the day and pay for a set lunch and high tea. Crates of bottled beer were carried on the coaches because many pubs along the way would have signs announcing that coach parties were not catered for. By the time they arrived, most beano parties were flushed and ready to enjoy themselves. The younger women would wear little sailor hats with legends such as *Kiss Me* on the brim. The men would have a flower in their button holes, and often new cloth caps. To watch them stumble aboard a boat was hilarious. Our mother used to frown, and say *I don't know what Hastings is coming to*. Apparently beano parties were supposed to go only to Southend or Margate, but I loved the clowning and the flamboyance of their half-tight condition. They were liberated. I can remember one man trying to do a sailor's hornpipe between the narrow thwarts and the women laughing and nudging each other. On another trip, in a cold wind, a man with no teeth sang *O Sol Mio* as if he was in a gondola in Venice on a soft languorous night. The others became serious or maudlin, and joined in the refrain.

The boat rides were special treats, one of the fixed landmarks of our holidays, but the beach had other attractions. One was the town crier. He wore a blue frock coat with gold braid, a cockaded top hat and a waistcoat with brass buttons. He would ring a bell and shout *O Yez* before announcing the municipal news such as the change of programmes at the Winter Garden or the local cinemas. Another was the Man in the Tub. He too wore a top hat, a battered one, and a long Victorian bathing costume. He would paddle along the beach in a big washtub, shouting jokes and every few minutes capsizing the tub before coming ashore to make a collection. As I recall, our mother gave him a penny every other day. Then there was Lobby Lud, who was employed by some newspaper to increase circulation. He would visit the seaside towns in turn, and his coming was widely advertised. If you recognized him from the indistinct picture published, carried a copy of the paper, and said *You are Lobby Lud, I claim the reward*, you got a quid or a pound. We never did, but his visit was always an exciting occasion.

Come lunchtime we would go to Reeves and I would have my roast beef and Yorkshire pud. We never went back to the beach in the afternoon no matter how fine the weather. Instead we would toil up the East or West Hill. The East Hill was my favourite, although I think our mother preferred the other when with the houses and passing traffic there was more to see. She would sit and knit, and Billie and I would clamber about the ruins of the castle. There was not much of it, but the weathered stone stood on downland turf and was very handsome. I would dream of wielding Weland's sword against the Winged Hats. At times I was the Centurion of the Thirtieth. The periods and locations were confused, but I enjoyed myself enormously. One year I took to Hastings a crusader shield I had made from cardboard and painted silver with a red cross. I thought this appropriate although William had landed at Hastings before the crusades. It was a great letdown, which somehow told against Hastings, when I discovered that he had killed Harold some miles inland, at a place subsequently named Battle, but the castle was still a wonderful place to play and dream in.

Our mother did not object to this fantasy. Rather she indulged me because for her it was history, and therefore to be encouraged. Which probably explains why one of the day trips we always made from Hastings was to Rye. It is a pleasant old walled town perched on a hill which once was a headland jutting into the Channel. The sea receded long ago, and the town now looks down on to saltings, or sea meadows. There is a splendid view from the church tower of the red-tiled houses and the River Rother winding through the saltings to the sea. The main attraction for our mother was that Rye was one of the Cinque Ports. I am not sure if she knew what this meant. I can't remember any explanation, but Rye was history to be enjoyed and appreciated. Every year we trailed through the narrow streets, and went to look at the *Mermaid*. This is a medieval inn standing on a steep cobbled lane. We never went inside. The women in twin sets and pearls and men in tweed or flannel suits were enough to warn us off, but one of the treats of Rye was tea in a shop near the church. The warming pans on the walls may have been bogus, but again this was a bit of Olde Englande we had been taught to admire. There were also jam tarts and shop cake to eat.

During the second week of the holiday we had the other set excursion, a mystery tour in a charabanc. They were old motor coaches with canvas roofs. Their vintage was also apparent because instead of one door into the coach with an aisle down the middle, the bench seats stretched the full width of the vehicle with little doors on both sides. The charas waited at the front near the clock tower with black-boards leaning against the brass radiators announcing the price and starting time. The latter was always approximate because as with the boats they would rarely start before they were full. They were wonderful outings, the like of which will probably never be enjoyed again. For a start, the charas were wonderful vehicles. The brass of the radiators and head-lamps was brightly polished, as were the hub caps and the buckles of the leather straps securing the canvas top. The ten or twelve little doors on each side also had brass handles. The solid rubber tires and the running board were white-washed. The paint was bright and spick and span, and each chara had its name—*Seagull* is one I can remember—painted in flowing characters on the back. The drivers wore peaked caps and goggles and long white dustcoats. They were old vehicles, even in those days. I suppose they were built soon after the first world war, but they were beautifully preserved and looked a treat lined up against the sea.

Most of them were supposed to start at seven in the evening, but it was generally half past before they moved off with a little round of ironic applause from the passengers. Everybody was in good humour. They had had their high teas, the heat of the day had gone and they were determined to enjoy themselves. There was no pretence. A chara ride was a rare treat. Apart from buses and beanos such excursions were the only times most people rode in a vehicle. Certainly it was the only ride we had in the year. If we were lucky we would sit up front with the driver. I would sit with my legs dangling and looking down from what seemed a great height at ordinary folk on the pavement as we drove out of town. I suppose this momentary feeling of superiority was rather horrid, but it doubled the enjoyment. For all those people knew, I went for a ride every night and always sat next to the driver.

Then there were few other cars, and the war and the depression had delayed urban sprawl. The main road quickly narrowed, and the lanes into which we turned were hardly wide enough for the chara. Apart from the macadamed surface they probably had remained unchanged since early Victorian times. We would bowl along at about twenty miles an hour looking over the hedgerows and *oohing* and *aahing* at the views and the cottages. The countryside was completely unspoilt, without power pylons and very few telephone lines. We rarely met another car. Apart from the occasional enamelled advertisement and *Hovis* signs outside general shops in the villages, I could have been sitting outside a stage coach next to Sam Weller if not Mr Pickwick himself.

These excursions were called mystery tours because no destination was announced. In fact, they were gentle drives through the countryside and a few villages, and eventually to a country pub. I think it was always the same pub. At least I have a strong memory of a typical Sussex ale house with a long low building behind in which were tables and benches for excursion parties. I can also remember the two-pronged attack or rush into the pub, one group rather desperately making for the lavatories and the other for the bar. Our mother would have a glass of port and lemon, which she sipped with the greatest delicacy. We would have ginger beer from stone bottles and sausage rolls. I can remember one evening when the beer and port and the fug of the pub had their inevitable effect upon the party after the cool, wind-swept drive. The thaw was quick and complete. There was first a buzz of conversation, and as the first cigarette smoke drifted up to the bare electric lights somebody strummed the piano. Very soon someone began to sing, and before the first refrain had finished everybody had joined in. We all knew the songs. Most of them were old music hall ditties passed down from parents to children. *We knocked them in the Old Kent Road, One of the ruins which Cromwell knocked about a* bit, *My dear old Dutch*, *There was I waiting at the church*, *A bicycle made for two* and many more. I knew all the words, and still do. Whatever their origins, they were genuine Cockney folk music, overly sentimental perhaps but expressing and reflecting communal attitudes.

The singing led to more rounds of drink, but before closing time the driver came in and there was another rush to the lavatories before climbing aboard. The return journey was in the dark of course. The wind was cold, providing sufficient excuse for young couples to cuddle together on the back benches. The singing resumed, this time of songs such as *A'roaming in the gloaming*. Sitting up front was like being in another world, a lighted tube through which we roared with the world outside unseen. I imagined I was Bulldog Drummond accelerating down the Dover Road in his Bentley to another improbable adventure and then Toad of Toad Hall. I did not see much difference between them. I did not know that Drummond was supposed to represent anti-Semitic and fascist tendencies of the island race, and I was also unaware that Toad was a figure of fun. I thought he was a spendid creature, adventurous and headstrong but kind-hearted.

The chara returned to the clock tower about eleven, and with my bare sun-tanned legs tingling in the night air we walked along the front back to Mrs Wilkins. The lights were on in the big hotels, and I could see the riding lights of some fishing boats. The sea was unseen, but I could hear the waves breaking on the beach below. They sounded better on Hastings shingle than on sand because the undertow carried some rattling pebbles with it. Mrs Wilkins let us in and offered tea, but I would stumble up to the top floor and without bothering to change into pyjamas fall into a dreamless sleep.

I suppose as with most children's holidays, at the beginning the fortnight would seem interminable. We could afford to waste time or accept rain uncomplainingly because there was always another day and then another. But half way through the second week the days would seem to rush by like the unseen world beyond the headlights of the chara. Our mother would think of going home and would buy small presents for Uncle Lou and Mary. This was compensation of a sort because it meant that we could go into shops with a purpose. We were able to, and about to spend money. It was not quickly spent. Our mother was not easily separated from money, and of course we enjoyed going into the little shops to compare mother-of-pearl trinket boxes with bits of pottery made in Rye and labelled *A Present from Hastings*. The last evening was always spent strolling along the promenade to the pier. I can remember being proud of my sun tan, and feeling both superior and jealous about the new arrivals with their pale skins. We would take what we knew was our last look at the front for another year with a proprietorial air. We belonged, with the better hotels, the other promenading families, the couples—the men in Oxford bags, blazers and neckerchiefs, the women with a woollen cardigan over their cotton frocks. We would pay our pennies and push through the heavy turnstiles on to the pier. I can still feel the warm planking through the rubber soles of my school plimsolls like the deck of a ship. Old people would sit in shelters muffled against the cool evening air, teenagers would be playing the pinball machines, but the sky and sea seemed limitless. There was the smell of adventure and the powerful feeling of the world beyond beckoning, but meanwhile here was Hastings, known, shabbily comfortable and safe. That last night was always infinitely sad, and the train journey home the next morning an anti-climax to be got over as quickly as possible.

I suppose we must have gone to Hastings nine or ten times when I was at school. The only time we went elsewhere was when I was fifteen, just before I went to work at *The Times*. A neighbour, a former naval petty officer who skippered a firefloat on the Thames, had a bungalow near Dymchurch in Kent which he offered to our mother for three guineas a week. The bungalow turned out to be an old converted railway carriage resting on railway sleepers in the sand. It was comfortable. At one end two of the compartments had been converted into bedrooms with bunk beds constructed from the cushioned bench seats. At the other end the last compartment was the kitchen. In between the compartment partitions had been removed making a large room with more cushioned bench seats round the sides. The one drawback was that it was like living in a glasshouse. Each of the many windows, some with *No Smoking* signs on them, was curtained but for privacy and not to keep the daylight out. We woke every morning at dawn. I did not mind much, but the inconvenience chipped a little of the complete confidence I had in our mother. Until then everything she said was gospel. She was the fount of most knowledge and all wisdom. For years, for as long as I could remember, she had said *I never sleep a wink at night*. But in those blinding dawns I awoke in the compartment which I shared with Billie to hear her gently snoring behind the partition in the space she shared with Beatie.

The last time I saw Dymchurch and neighbouring Camber Sands they had become shantytowns. Other people had built rather nasty little bungalows on the cheap sandy land. But then the man who owned our railway carriage was a pioneer. The area was relatively uncluttered and was as beautiful as most coastal flatlands. Romney Marsh had long been drained, but the roads were narrow with angular bends. The meadows were lush and used for sheep grazing. The sea was kept back by a seawall, behind which crouched Martello towers built to stop Napoleon's armies from landing. Beyond were sand dunes and miles of clean sandy beaches. It was a splendid place for a children's holiday, but we were not altogether happy. We missed Hastings, the promenade and the streets. We were urban animals uneasy when there was no pavement under our feet. The wail of the gulls was attractive at first, but we missed the constant background of city sounds and noises. We did not admit it to each other, but were happier than usual to return to Shadwell.

But after every holiday our mother used to say, *It's nice to be home again*. And it was. It was nice to see Mary again, and Uncle Lou, Tom and Jim. It was hardly nice, but nevertheless pleasurable to compare my sun tan with the pale skin of the kids who had not been on holiday. Of course, I missed the sea and the castle ruins on the East Hill, but such memories faded quicker than the sun tan. And Shadwell was not drab during the summer months. The funnels and superstructure of the ships above the dock wall could be bright in the sun, which would also catch the wake of ships and lighters moving on the river. Even the lighters, the coffin-like barges which often just floated with the tide steered by a long oar, looked better. The hulls were tarred, but the hatch copings were painted with red primary paint. The streets were alive with traffic and people during the day. They were quiet in the evening, but not deserted. Families would bring out kitchen chairs and sit on the pavement. Our mother never did. She was always for keeping herself to herself. She used to say of the neighbours that they were driven out by fleas, which was probably true. Certainly I used to find the occasional bed bug on our sheets although they were regularly washed, one a week with the clean sheet always going underneath.

Whatever the reason, the little groups outside most doors made for a friendly atmosphere. The mothers would watch the children playing in the deserted road—there were no lorries or carts after the dock gates closed at five. In some groups would be an old granny, bent and gnarled, with a thin white bun of hair protruding from her man's cap. The men would often sit on the curb, with their feet in the gutter. Occasionally one of them would take a jug to the *Lovat* for a quart of mild beer which they would drink out of jam jars. The women never smoked, but the men would fill stubby little clay pipes or roll cigarettes. Sometime in the early evening the brush and pan artist would work his way along the street. He was a council man employed to remove the horse droppings in the middle of the road, which without stooping he did with a long-handled brush and pan. Later the water cart would come along washing the trash and dust into the gutters. Many of the kids who did not wear shoes would run behind gambolling in the spray from the long sprinkler. I always wanted to but our mother never let us out of the house without shoes. The men sitting on the curb would get up slowly and almost too late as the cart went by and shout good-naturedly at the driver. About half past eight Mary would call me in. Often the family would be sitting in the shop with the door open and watching the street outside, but the light would be switched on in the dining room for supper. Afterwards I would want to go out again, but permission was rarely given. Reluctantly I would go up to my bedroom, and undressing would watch the lights opposite being switched on. Then to bed to listen to the river noises as I fell asleep. Yes, it was nice to be home again.

# 5

THE EAST End attracted many charitable organizations in those days. The best known in Stepney was Toynbee Hall, and there were the university settlement houses. Charitable work was done by the churches, and Wapping was not the only neighbourhood with its permanent mission. Some were supported by temperance societies. I remember one in St George's near St Katherine's Dock clearly because of the very graphic posters displayed outside the chapel-like premises. The theme was *Before and After*, and the posters showed in great detail the domestic life of a family before and after the father took to drink. I was strongly affected, especially by the last picture showing the mother with a baby in her arms and other children clutching her long skirts being turned out of her house while the drunken father slept it off in the gutter. I many times swore never to touch a drop, a pledge which I am happy to report was not observed. Apart from the permanent missions, the churches and chapels had visiting missions once a year. The Catholics had special missionary orders, and St Mary and St Michael's would be crowded when they came with their own variety of fire and brimstone.

I have the impression now that in spite of the evident need for help the clerical and lay organizations did very little except preach. Toynbee Hall might have been different, but Whitechapel was not our neighbourhood. The settlement houses might have provided useful social therapy for well-to-do undergraduates, but they did not much help the local inhabitants. One year a group of them decided to perform their good works in the church hall of St Paul's. It was an event, announced by the vicar from the pulpit after the banns of marriage. I heard afterwards that they came from his old Oxford college, which may have explained his enthusiasm. Whatever the reason, it was contagious and I looked forward to the first night with the greatest expectation.

St Paul's church hall was a building better than most of its kind. Probably built in the early 19th century, it was a long two-storey building with good Georgian proportions and with not too much stucco to look tatty about a century later. The lower two floors each had an auditorium or hall with smaller rooms at each end. These were used by the Sunday school, which had three or four classes, and by various groups during the week. We registered in one of the halls for the new whatever-it-was the Oxbridge chaps had to give us. When my turn came one of them asked me for my name, address and age. He then asked me what my father did for a living. I said that he was dead, that I was an orphan. I'm fairly certain it was the first time I had used the word. I was not certain whether you could be an orphan with only one parent dead. Certainly I had never thought of myself as one, but the situation seemed to demand it. I rather enjoyed feeling sorry for myself until the Oxbridge man became wet-eyed. Apparently he was overcome by the pity of it, of not only growing up in a slum but being an orphan too.

This may sound very grown-up, but I was not the wordly, sophisticated slum kid the situation may suggest. I was in fact rather Boy-Scoutish. I was by nature enthusiastic. I expected to be done good to, as much as I expected to do good to others. I believed in the Lord's Prayer, goodness, honesty, hard work and opportunity. In the American experience, I was cast in the Horatio Alger mould. Our mother, Uncle Lou and Mary had strongly conditioned me. Most of all our mother, who had a very strong sense of personally belonging. For her, patriotism was personal. She believed in the monarchy, the church and the Empire because she saw herself as part of it. This explained her classlessness, and mine. In the circumstances I was later willing to make allowances kindly. That undergraduate was after all a stranger. He was nice, at least to me. His presence at St Paul's established his good intentions. He was, I suppose, nineteen or twenty years old. He had no side, no indication of assumed superiority in spite of his accent and well-cut tweeds. I wish him well if he is still alive. He would be sixty if he survived the war, and he looked the kind who would have joined a good fighting regiment. But for all the good he intended, he might as well have been a Victorian missionary of the strict Nonconformist school and Shadwell a Polynesian island. The gulf between us was in fact wider. Presumably Victorian missionaries offered rudimentary medicine and the safety match as well as Christianity. He and his friends had really nothing to give or teach.

I don't think that the gulf was a matter of class attitudes entirely, but between two utterly foreign ways of life. He and his friends must have felt alien and lost in Shadwell as years later I felt alien and lost arriving in Haifa at the height of the Jewish-Palestinian Arab struggle. I had flown in aboard what was to be the last KLM flight before general war began. From Amsterdam to Athens the Dakota, or DC3, was full of Jewish immigrants, most of them from refugee camps, and a few American Zionists. At Athens we were told that Haifa airport was silent. Nobody knew if it had been destroyed or had become a battlefield. After explaining this the pilot, an Englishman, said that the company had contracted to take us to Haifa and was willing to fulfil its part if at all possible, but at our own risk. I was the only foreign correspondent on board, and perhaps foolishly the only passenger who felt obliged to take that risk. Soon after I took off in an empty plane, except for the crew, and sat at the back with the Dutch steward drinking beer and Bols gin until Mount Carmel was sighted. The plane circled over the city. We could see the smoke of war on Carmel and in some parts of the town, but the airfield was undamaged if still silent.

We landed, and taxied right up to the terminal building without seeing anybody. The steward opened the door, put down a little ladder, and after I had climbed down handed me my grip and typewriter. Then as an afterthought he tossed down three or four small bottles of Bols, and waved. The plane turned and immediately took off. I was utterly alone, a condition which did not change much when I met a Jewish policeman inside the terminal. He was dressed in the usual British colonial police uniform, spoke English and was reasonably polite but had already become an Israeli. Whatever relationship the British and Palestinian Jews had had previously, and it was closer than many imagined at the time, we were already alien to each other. I soon learned my way about, of course. Israel remained foreign, but no more than any other country in my reportorial career after I had made acquaintances, mastered the politics and got used to the cigarettes. But that night in St Paul's church hall I sensed, or knew, that those nice men would always be alien to Shadwell. They would never have made friends or acquaintances, and judging from subsequent reading of magazines such as the *New Statesman* they would never have mastered the politics.

Perhaps I'm being unfair. I can remember the Oxbridge chap as if it was yesterday. He had a soft almost foolish face behind his horn-rimmed spectacles, a face relaxed by material well-being and security. His tweeds were greeny-grey, and his necktie had a repetitive insignia which years afterwards I learned to recognize as a college tie. This I can remember, but of course I did not know him. Nevertheless, he made no further impression upon me or the parish, and quickly disappeared with the others. But from all the available indications, from then until now, his like had no idea of our politics or of what we thought. Only recently I read a front-page article in the *New Statesman*, the first after Tony Howard had become editor, entitled *What about the workers*. What indeed! There was nothing in the piece to suggest that the writer knew about them, or really cared for them.

The Oxbridge chap presumably cared, in the inane American sense of the word, but had no idea of what to do. Which was a pity. We were not the helpless slum kids of popular imagination. We had goodish schools and libraries, we enjoyed ourselves, and in the background was the strong sense of Labour politics and the trade union movement. Above all, we shared a very civilized social relationship, no doubt nurtured by necessity, but all the stronger for that. We were isolated of course, but given a little notice or encouragement the United Kingdom could have been united. Instead, Disraeli's two Englands remained very much apart. The charitable work intended to bridge the gulf, at a humane if not economic level, failed. It was cold, indifferent and uncomprehending as were the social policies of the then government. One reason I suppose was that most of the charitable groups had long lost their original enthusiasm. All that remained were the buildings, decrepit and run down for lack of money and true intention. They were organization without life. The one surviving enthusiasm was for self-denial on our part, mainly drink. The reasons why the poor drank, and they were not all explained by socio-economic conditions, were apparently never examined. As for the young Oxbridge types, clearly they had never thought out why they visited Shadwell and what they could usefully do there.

For all the disappointment, the church remained one of the main focal points of my life. Apart from serving at the altar and singing in the choir, we had choir practice twice a week which were also social occasions. I also belonged to the Boys' Brigade for a time. I can remember little of it now except for the uniform, dark-blue woollen shirt, shorts and forage cap. Presumably the vicar thought it would be good for us, but as with the Oxbridge chaps he had given no thought to what we wanted. I can now vaguely recall church parades and learning First Aid, but nothing more. All this helps to explain why the 2nd City of London Sea Scout Troop played such an important part in my young life.

I suppose most scout troops then were similar to the Boys' Brigade, a kind of hangover of an Edwardian assumption that military discipline and fresh air were good for boys. The scouts probably offered more in the way of camping, but most were attached to churches or chapels. I would guess that the vast majority were led by well-meaning people who had not much idea of what to do with children except for the hope of keeping them out of trouble. The 2nd City of London was entirely different. If I was still a betting man— I gave up poker after the arrival of my first child—I would make a small wager that it was unique. It was not attached to a church. Mr Thomas, the scout master, was a very Welsh-looking Welshman who remained in the background to attend to business requiring the attention of an adult. Otherwise the troop was run by the members. It was a kibbutz, kongsi or commune of boys, an extraordinary self-governing, self-motivating and self-perpetuating group. They numbered about twenty, and the age groups were from about twelve to eighteen. Presumably the older boys had their own interests and relationship, but I was deeply involved with about half-a-dozen other boys for three years until I was sixteen or seventeen.

The headquarters when I joined was in a derelict office building in Crutched Friars in the City of London. It was a short street off Seething Lane and behind Trinity Square. Fenchurch Street railway station was built over one end of the street. I can't recall going there during a working day, and so for me it was always a quiet little street deserted except for the occasional policeman or caretaker. No 23 Crutched Friars was a four-storey building, empty except for the second floor where the troop met. The occupancy was temporary, until the building was demolished to make way for a new office block but there was little building in those depressed days. The headquarters comprised a large open space in front, and three rooms at the side and behind the stairwell. One was used as an office by the scoutmaster and another was reserved for the older boys. The third eventually became the office of the *Red Duster*, a cyclostyled four-page magazine I put out at infrequent intervals. The whole place was badly lighted, tatty and impossible to keep clean. Dust and soot seeped in through the window frames and came out of the walls and ceiling. The only furniture we had were three tables and some chairs, the only equipment a ping-pong table.

The troop came from all over London. Mr Thomas, a civil servant and bachelor, for a time lived in a flat at the top of a warehouse in Upper Thames Street. Jack Kelly came from the Old Kent Road and Jim Rodgers from Museum Street in Bloomsbury where his father kept a newsagent's shop. The Shadwell contingent, apart from myself, included Mr Higgins, the assistant scout master who lived in West Garden Buildings opposite, and Dave Cleaver, who lived in Bewley Buildings behind the shop. One of the older boys, whose name I have forgotten, came from Hoxton, which then had the reputation of being the toughest neighbourhood in East London. He rode a Norton 500 c.c. motorcycle which I envied. He killed himself one day overtaking a tram when another was coming from the opposite direction. We were all poor but none so poverty-stricken as Jack Kelly. His mother was also a widow, but did not have a shop and had to go out to work. I believe that she had two or three other children. Jack was the eldest and worked as a french polisher, and his hands were always stained and filthy. He was painfully thin and had bad teeth, but he was the wit of the troop. He had true Cockney wit, quick and sharp, self-mocking and derisive of all authority. Inevitably he set the mood of our small group, and the older boys were wary of him.

We were an odd lot, who had become sea scouts because there was no other way of getting near a boat. Not that we did much boating or sailing at first. The troop did not then have a boat, but Mr Thomas owned what we grandly called a motor cruiser. It was a converted ship's lifeboat, which could sleep six at a pinch. The *Lady Molly*, as she was called, was usually kept in a mud berth at Benfleet, behind Canvey Island in Essex. The water was so shallow that except at spring tides she only floated four or five hours on each tide. We could only go down at weekends, and then about once a month because each member of the troop had to have his turn. We could not have gone down more often in any case because of the expense. Scouts were given a very cheap rate by the railway when travelling in groups, but none of us could afford to go to Benfleet very often. Theoretically this meant that we could expect about six weekends afloat every spring and summer, but the tides made this impossible. About twice a year I spent the weekend on the mud hoping without reason that the tide would rise before nightfall.

But even the weekends on the mud could be fun. The main cabin was cosy, especially at night when we lighted the Tilley lamp. The layout was basic to all small boats. Along each side was a cushioned bench, which became a bunk at night. Down the middle was a let-down table hinged to the centreboard casing. The galley was to the right of the companion way leading to the cockpit. It was simple, a small sink, a primus stove and two cupboards for food and crockery. Our taste in food was no less simple, eggs and bacon, beef sausages because they were cheaper than pork, bread and jam, and tea. All this, including some bottled beer and a few cigarettes, cost each of us about two shillings. The typical supper was sausages, fried tomato, potatoes and bread, and mugs of tea sweetened with condensed milk as well as sugar. When we felt flush we would have a tin of peaches or pineapple with condensed milk for afters. I suppose it was an unhealthy diet, but the grease kept us warm and provided almost instant energy. Presumably this is why the food of the poor or in poor areas in meat-eating countries all over the world is so greasy.

I was reminded of this years later in the American deep south. I was with Martin Luther King Jr. on his 1961 freedom ride, and the church in which he preached in Montgomery, Alabama, was attacked. This led to a stopover of three or four days, during which several well-meaning whites, in spite of all the evidence, sought to persuade me that their niggers—or rather, nigras—were happy, well loved, and free to do whatever they wanted. One of the whites, a dignified old gentleman who looked as if he had wandered off a

Hollywood set while playing the role of a southern senator, took me to a restaurant for some real, good southern-fried chicken. I was served two or three pieces of chicken, greens, fried-over potatoes and grits, and was just about to eat when the cook emerged carrying a heavy iron skillet. *Fresh grease tonight*, he said with pride, and poured what appeared to be a quarter pint of grease over my food. I demurred, but my host took my protestations as so much English, or southern, good manners. Southerners, essentially poor and hard working in spite of their aristocratic posturing, needed greasy food as much as we did in Shadwell.

It was doubly necessary aboard the *Molly*, except at the height of summer. We could work up a good fug with after-supper cigarettes and the Tilley lamp roaring, but of the crew of six two had to sleep in the fo'c'sle and another two in the open cockpit under an awning. It could be very cold with only one blanket and an oilskin, and was always dank. Benfleet was also a bleak place. Perched on the edge of the Essex marshes, Canvey Island provided some protection from the estuary, but there was nothing to stop the wind. The general impression was of low sea walls, cheap bungalows and an immense sky. The immediate and constant impression was of mud. The channel between Benfleet and the island was basically a mud gully which the tide briefly covered twice a day. During these short periods there would be frantic activity as boats sped to the open estuary. Then, seemingly in a flash, the water would disappear revealing vast expanses of mud with a winding narrow strip of water down the middle. On more than one occasion we misjudged the tide and were left marooned on a mud bank. There was no harbour, basin or marina. The boats were tied to the bank and anchored aft, and spent about two-thirds of their time on mud.

It was a ridiculous place to keep a boat, except to lay up in winter, but of course it was cheap. I could not have hoped to sail a boat without belonging to the sea scouts, and the City of London troop, or rather Mr Thomas, could not have kept the *Molly* except in a place such as Benfleet where an anchorage cost only a few quid a year. The entire area apparently existed on this kind of equation. The boats were all conversion jobs like the *Molly*, and some so amateurishly done that they must have been unsafe to move in a high wind. The *Molly* was a workmanlike boat. The cabin roof had been raised only about fifteen inches amidships and the deck was uncluttered except for a small skylight. She was yawl-rigged which meant that the open cockpit aft could hold half-a-dozen people without fear of having their heads knocked off by the mizzen-mast boom. Some of the other boats had very high cabin roofs, presumably to give six feet or more head-room below, wheelhouses and other naval architectural structures most unsuited for small boats. The carpentry was no less amateurish. The bungalow-dwellers were there because the land was cheap, and many of the bungalows looked as gimcrack and absurd as the boats.

Years afterwards I was marooned in Basra for 36 hours because the BOAC plane I had boarded at Tokyo, after covering the Korean war, developed engine trouble just before take-off. I sat in the bar with an oilman who said that Basra was the arsehole of the world. He went on to say that Baghdad was 500 miles up it, and immediately I thought of Benfleet. It was the arsehole of the Thames. But it was all we could afford, and with this accepted a mutual compensating mechanism came into play. We compared Benfleet with Burnham, if not Cowes. Somehow we saw Benfleet as part of the entire Essex coast although we saw very little of it. Which was a pity, because it is, or was, lovely in its bleak loneliness.

In those days, of course, boating was not the popular pastime it is now. With the possible exception of sailing dinghies there were no mass-produced boats. We would read about hand-built boats in the back numbers of *Yachting World* which Jim Rodgers used to sneak out of his father's shop. We would marvel over the detailed drawings, and dream of sailing away in these masterpieces to the South Seas, but a ship's lifeboat, converted or ready for conversion, was all that was available. We therefore applied the same compensating mechanism to the *Molly*, and in fact she was not a bad boat. She was at least stoutly built, seaworthy and cheap. We kept her in good trim, and the paintwork and brass were always clean. In retrospect, Benfleet had similar advantages apart from cheapness. The sky was the main one. It was huge because of the flatness of the land. Even when the *Molly* was stuck in the mud, the scudding clouds gave me a sensation of movement. But after the narrow horizon of the tenements and dock walls of Shadwell, the sheer size of the Benfleet sky was the greatest sensation. The cleanness of the light almost routed the smell of mud, but it always seemed dank. Mud oozed into rubber boots and rain down the collar of oil-skins. The damp penetrated everything, especially the old Morris Marine engine mounted partly under the floorboards of the cockpit. It was built before batteries became common in boats, and had a magneto instead of coil ignition. The magneto was nearly always damp, and I took it to bed with me one night to dry. No luck, my blanket was as damp as the bilge under the floorboards. No wonder that we tucked into greasy food. One night in early spring, when we had gone down to paint the *Molly* before the sailing season, I was so cold that I spread margarine thickly onto a piece of fried bread dripping with bacon fat.

Benfleet was not our only weekend escape from Shadwell.

We also went to Greenhithe, which was further up the river on the Kent shore. The troop had some tenuous connection with the *Worcester*, a training ship for merchant navy cadets. We did not go on the ship, an old square-rigger anchored offshore. I think we were regarded as not good enough to mix with the cadets. A second mate's or master's ticket in the merchant navy does not of course have the same social importance as a commission in the navy, but most of the *Worcester* cadets were bound for the P & O and other large shipping lines. They looked solid middle class in their midshipman's uniforms. We envied as much as we disparaged them. I used to associate them with Peter Kelso in the Percy F. Westerman books, and would think of them reporting with their seachests to the good ship *Golden Hope*. But we saw them from a distance because we were only allowed to camp on some ground the *Worcester* owned above the village.

Again it was hardly a salubrious area. The local cement factories coated the village and what was left of its surrounding with fine white-grey dust. There was not much left of the surroundings because of the worked-out quarries. The camping ground was no bigger than a couple of tennis courts, and was perched above a deep railway cutting. But again our compensating mechanism did the trick and transformed it into a sylvan glade. Actually it was not the rural slum it could have been. The rain washed the cement dust into the chalk and flint soil. The grass survived because we were the only people to use the camping ground. The railway cutting, which had been abandoned, led into a series of quarries which were wonderful places to explore. A small copse yielded sufficient fuel for our cooking fire. We also attracted the local girls who were far more complaisant than those I knew in Shadwell. Because of them I grew up convinced that country girls had the morals and appetites of goats. In comparison the Shadwell girls were paragons of virtue.

Greenhithe was a three-hour bicycle ride from Crutched Friars. We used to go over Tower Bridge, down the Old Kent Road to Deptford and Blackheath, and then along the old A2. By then I had begun work, and had bought the bike through what I think was called the Sundry Publications Dept of *The Times*. The main purpose of the department was to sell copies of the paper's then much-admired photographs, but it also ran a cut-rate purchasing scheme for the staff. Through it I bought a James bicycle for £3. 2s. 6d., a saving, as I recall, of 15 shillings. I bought it on the instalment plan, paying 2s. 6d. a week. It was a handsome machine with a blue-enamelled frame, racing handle bars and a big touring bag strapped to the back of the saddle. On the trips to Greenhithe I would sling two old army packs from the carrier, one each side of the rear wheel.

Apart from the obvious attraction of the girls, I suppose that I preferred Greenhithe to Benfleet. It was cheaper for a start because Benfleet was too far from Shadwell to bike comfortably. Greenhithe was space, well relative space. Sleeping in a two-man tent was preferable to the cockpit or fo'c'sle of the *Molly*. At least it was easier to relieve yourself in the copse than in a bucket. I liked the *Molly* although she could be a very stationary boat. Whoever coined the phrase *mucking about in boats* knew what he was talking about, but at Greenhithe we did real sailing. The *Worcester* had a small fleet of old naval whalers and we were allowed to use one of them when the ship was closed for the summer holidays.

The old whaler was a very good boat, seaworthy and almost non-capsizable. Rather more than 20 feet overall, it was double-ended and equipped with a centreboard. It was a bit heavy for five boys to row, and could not sail close to the wind. There was no cabin. Nevertheless, designed as an all-purpose boat for naval ships and built to last, it was as perfect an example of utilitarian beauty as the jeep in the second world war. The naval routine of the *Worcester* ensured that the whaler made available to us was always shipshape, scrubbed, polished and with no loose ends. The knowledge that all Royal Navy ships carried whalers, and that they were rowed and sailed on every sea, increased the attraction. The whaler had a powerful and unexpected effect upon us. Unused as we were to the para-military discipline affected by most scout troops, we were nevertheless always galvanized into displays of disciplined crewmanship when aboard. Our language became very nautical. We said *Aye, aye* at the smallest excuse. We always wore our uniforms.

The sea scout uniform was in fact practical, comfortable and quite smart—a round sailor cap, navy-blue jersey with the legend *Sea Scouts* embroidered in white across the chest, a blue and white neckerchief and blue shorts—but we rarely wore it because of the neighbourhoods in which we lived. Such a get-up aroused ridicule and sly humour. Also we were not the types to wear uniform gladly. I am writing of the years immediately before the second world war when blackshirts and greenshirts were beginning to be worn. As a group we were not politically conscious. Unbelievably some of the boys were Tories, but we instinctively rebelled against the idea of wearing a uniform—except aboard that whaler.

Greenhithe is on Long Reach, which as the name suggests is a longish and straight stretch of water. It is no more attractive than Benfleet creek. Alas, unlike Rio de Janeiro, San Francisco and New York, the seaward approach to London is uniformly dull. It is relieved a bit at Long Reach by the sight of Kentish hills behind, but the northern bank is a grim sea wall, sloping and rather treacherous for small boats. In those days the monotony was only broken by an isolation hospital. But there was plenty of water for sailing. Even with a clumsy sailer such as a whaler, one could always hope for long tacks and fair speed. The only obstacles were the ships passing to and from London. They could also be dangerous as we discovered one grey and blowy Saturday morning.

We were running free with the wind and tide behind us when a big freighter came round the bend. She was heavily laden and moving faster than us. I had read the rule of the road at sea, and knew that steam is supposed to give way to sail. I held course convinced that the skipper or pilot knew the rules, but either he did not or had decided that they did not apply to small boats. She came on, her black bow growing more and more huge and threatening. I could hear her screws thrashing as if she was battling the monsoon in the Bay of Bengal. I looked up and could see no face. She appeared to be as deserted as the *Marie Celeste*. I panicked, but fortunately did the right thing. I came about, and we were just about to pull away slowly when she blanketed the wind. We wallowed desperately in her wake. A couple of oars were quickly got out and the boat was held steady until the sails filled again, but I have never forgotten that freighter bearing down on me.

The Greenhithe weekends became less frequent when the troop moved from Crutched Friars to Scott's *Discovery*. She had been refurbished and moored at the Victoria Embankment, near the Temple, as a memorial to the explorer, but we were allowed to use it as a headquarters. It was an imaginative decision, whoever was responsible. He might have been the retired admiral we called on at Christmas. My imagination, already lively, was further fueled. I did not much like Scott and most of his brother officers and gentlemen after reading the socially superior explanation of Petty Officer Evans' collapse, but illogically admired Captain Oates. He especially provided an aura of high endeavour, gallantry and tragedy to what was a splendid ship and headquarters. From the deck we could see the noble sweep of the Embankment, with the Palace of Westminster to the west and St Paul's cathedral to the east. We were supposed only to use the main cabin, but quickly came to terms with the two naval pensioners who were the caretakers. We worked hard at it by doing much of the cleaning and polishing they were paid to do, but it was worthwhile. They taught us to splice and much else. One of them was very good with small boats, and taught us how to handle them safely on the fast tides of the narrowed river. We also got to know the river police, who would occasionally tow us back to the *Discovery*'s moorings when we had misjudged the tide.

Amazingly, the independence and internal anarchy of the troop remained unimpaired by our new surroundings. Whichever authority was responsible for the ship, we were never interfered with. As before, Mr Thomas remained in the background, generally in one of the small cabins off the main cabin. This was the area of the ship where members of the expedition had been quartered. The main cabin was largely filled by a big table and bolted-down chairs. To port and starboard were the sleeping cabins, each with built-in bunk and furniture. The woodwork was solid and beautifully constructed: the paintwork spick and span. It was far superior to the homes we came from. I don't think we were objectively aware of this, but the very solidity of the ship was comforting.

I realize now how lucky we were. Only recently I left Printing House Square after the six o'clock editorial conference to go to an embassy party and inserted my car into the lanes of traffic moving slowly westwards. There was a jam and I could see the *Discovery* ahead through the trees. In the other cars were men impatient to get home, those in the Jaguars and Rolls to expensive villas in the Thames valley perhaps. Presumably they were to be envied, but they could not have spent their evenings in a more satisfying place than we kids from Shadwell, the Old Kent Road and Hoxton did so many years ago. I now can't think of any place in London, New York, Singapore, Berlin or Cairo—to mention but a few of the cities I have enjoyed myself in—more satisfying than the *Discovery* before the war. It was wonderful.

We met two evenings a week, Tuesday and Friday, as well as at the weekend. I would have tea at home, and to save money would again walk to the Minories Underground station—past those *Before and After* posters—and ride to Blackfriars for two old pennies. Then there would be the walk along the Embankment and under the plane trees to the *Discovery*. The City would have emptied by that time. The posh chaps were back home in Hampstead, Highgate, Kensington, Holland Park or the outer suburbs. The less posh would be having their supper in Streatham, Fulham and Golders Green. Apart from the really posh chaps staying at the Savoy, it was ours, all ours. And our view was better than that from the Savoy. The best evenings were when the tide was just on the turn, and we would go up river to Chelsea bridge and beyond, or down to the Tower or lower to Shadwell New Park. We came to learn almost every inch of the river, and to be expert when needs be in working against the five- or six-knot current. Without a word of command from the man at the tiller we would work our way under the bridges or into the dead water behind moored lighters or piers. The final accolade came when the river police became less nosey and tugboat men would take a line from us. We belonged.

I can remember one evening when we paused at the top of the tide above Westminster Bridge. Some of us wanted to lay over to the south side, to St Thomas's hospital where some nurses could be seen, but to avoid a coalboat going up to Lambeth power station we pulled over towards the House of Commons. The terrace was crowded, and a few people, presumably Members or their guests, waved. I suppose that they were just enjoying the soft warm evening as we were, but we had read about strawberries and cream served on the terrace and Kelly made some disparaging remark. Then he stood up, and shouted, *Up the workers, the starving workers*. The people on the terrace laughed, and a few held up drinks. It was an amiable moment, but for some unknown reason is linked in my mind with a memory of an evening during the war.

I have forgotten where, but we were sitting in a ditch waiting to move forward. It was getting dark, and we were tired, cold and hungry. A Humber staff car came up the road quickly and suddenly stopped. A rear window was lowered, and a captain wearing a Rifle Brigade cap waved me peremptorily to the car. I got up creaking with the cold, and the heat from within the car enveloped my half-frozen unshaved face. He wanted to know the way to some headquarters I had not even heard about. I shook my head, probably looking stupid, but I was only aware of that warmth. Beyond the captain was a brigadier wearing a sheepskin jerkin over a tailored battledress. He had a red face and a little mouth with rodent-like teeth. He spoke sharply, and then from behind me came a concerted shout of *Food, food, we want Food*. Then *Fuck off, fuck off*. I was nonplussed and a bit frightened. After all, I was the only man standing in full view, and I saw the sergeant moving away. For a moment I thought that the captain or brigadier would strike me, but suddenly the window was wound up, the warmth disappeared and the car roared on.

Heaven knows why the two memories are linked. There was nothing bitter about the first. In those days or evenings on the river we did not feel bitter about anything or anybody. Only condescending. The river and the city were ours, as it could be for few other people. Silly nonsense of course. We did not even own the boat we rowed. We could have been kicked off the *Discovery* at any time. We would have had no redress. As it was, unknown and unseen authorities, apparently benign although it cost them nothing, let us have the use first of No 23 Crutched Friars and then the *Discovery*. Mr Thomas hovered in the background, apparently not doing anything and certainly not getting in our way. We were very lucky. Occasionally unseen forces intruded. There was a time when Mr Thomas required us, a bit shame-facedly as I recall, to attend church parades once a month at St Stephen's, Walbrook, just behind the Mansion House. I did not mind. St Stephen's is a lovely Wren church and the choir was worth listening to, but I never understood why we had to go. We also looked ridiculous because we knew neither drill not our left feet from our right. Our raggedness was all the more obvious when we lined up in the quiet City street deserted except for the well-to-do congregation watching curiously. Mr Thomas wore a peaked cap and managed to look like a deckchair attendant in one of the parks. The vicar ignored us, but I suppose we had to go to satisfy somebody in the city corporation.

Our relations with the other scout troops in the City of London were hardly close. We all wore a patch on our sleeves bearing the coat of arms of the City, and of which I was snobbishly proud, but we had nothing more in common. The self-appointed leaders were the 1st City of London. They were ordinary scouts, or land scouts as were the other troops, but clearly believed that they were the model for us all. They were attached to All Hallows-by-the-Tower. The vicar then was the Rev. Tubby Clayton, founder of Toc H and a fashionable and good priest. It was obviously a rich living, and the vicarage and church hall were in Trinity Square just round the corner from Crutched Friars. I have no idea where the boys came from, but they all looked middle class. Their uniforms were impeccable even down to the uniform brogues. The uniform was black, and we made the inevitable comparison with the Hitler Youth which must have been unfair. In any case, they were closer to the MRA (Moral Rearmament). They had the smug well-being of MRA-ers, secure within a wealthy organization as well as with God. I suppose I am still being unfair. I knew none of them individually. For me they were always an impersonal group, an establishment scout troop. They were attached to a well-heeled church, which postulated the masculine Christianity of Toc H. They went to Gilwell, the national camping ground of the movement. They went through Baden Powell's *Jungle Book* nonsenses with earnest jollity. They were horrible.

They were most horrid at the occasional get-togethers of City of London scout troops, which were held in their hall. Unlike Crutched Friars, it was heated, and the atmosphere of assured affluence reminded me of earlier visits to our Uncle Archie in Canning Town, except that their welcome was more effusive. We had the feeling that they had been told to be nice to us poor slum kids. Their activities and general behaviour suggested that we were being shown how a scout troop should be run. They did all the things scouts were supposed to do indoors from the *Jungle Book* stuff to part songs, which they sang like a well-rehearsed choir. *Father O'Flynn* was a great favourite. They all sang with exaggerated Irish accents, but made the wayward old reprobate sound like Mr Chips. Nevertheless, it could be galling, and eventually we decided to show them. From somewhere Mr Thomas borrowed a breeches-buoy, or life-saving apparatus, and we constructed a play round a display of life-saving. Because of my known connection with *The Times* and editorship of the *Red Duster*, I was nominated chief scriptwriter.

The opening scene was inside a hut on the Essex coast. A gale was raging outside, and we staggered into the hut as if we had just that minute returned from feats of endurance and high bravery. We removed our dripping oilskins—wettened from a fire bucket before coming on stage—and flung ourselves into poses of exhaustion about a table. We lighted cigarettes, drank what was supposed to be whisky, and talked of the horrors outside. These were implied rather than explained. Rather cleverly, I thought, I left to the audience to decide whether it was a Loch Ness Monster or another Flood. Kelly provided light relief. In a direct steal from a W. C. Fields film, he frequently opened the door and said, *It's not a fit night for men or beast*. A half-bucket of water was then thrown in his face. The first curtain was dramatic. One of the younger boys, in oilskins too long for him, rushed in shouting, *The Spray's on the Buxey*! We all recoiled in horror. *Not the Buxey! Not that graveyard of ships —And of men*! shrilled Kelly who now had to drop his comic role. The curtain came down as we all rushed off to save the crew of the good ship *Spray* aground on the most treacherous shoal in the Thames estuary.

So far so good, or so we thought. The second act, which

was to bring the house down, was the life-saving display. To raise the level of drama, and to get a few laughs, I had the *Spray* crewed by girls. About half a dozen of the younger ones were dressed in female finery, mainly nightgowns and bed caps because we could not afford wigs. Unfortunately this left us with too few to handle the heavy gear. I thought that the intense atmosphere I had so cleverly built-up was somewhat dissipated by setting up the gear in full view. The audience, who had been sitting in a half circle also had to move back to leave the middle of the hall clear. Finally the tripod was set up in the doorway at the back, and a line thrown to the poor girls clutching each other in terror on the stage. They swayed from side to side to give the impression of a rocking boat, and buckets of water were splashed from the wings. After a good deal of heaving and ho-ing we managed to rescue one girl, and there was a loud cheer as she glided the length of the hall in the buoy. A second was half way across when the gear collapsed and literally brought down the curtain. The evening as well as the play came to a quick chaotic end. Whoever it was emptying the firebuckets in the wings had been much too enthusiastic. Water slopped everywhere, and two or three boys fell as the audience stampeded. We were too dismayed to giggle. After all the reputation of the 2nd City of London was at stake, and the black-uniformed creeps in the 1st were more condescendingly MRA-ish than ever. The scoutmaster, a parson, made a short speech saying how hard we had tried, and they gave us three cheers. We could have killed them.

Nevertheless, some of us went round to St Hallows church hall regularly in the winter to talk with a young curate. I have forgotten his name, which is a pity. Although he was not much older than the Oxbridge chaps who had come to St Paul's he was everything they were not. There was no unbridgeable gulf. He understood us, or at least bore with us. We spent many evenings in his rooms in Trinity Square. They were warm, carpeted, booklined and very comfortable. He would sit at a big desk while we sprawled in easy chairs or on the rug in front of the fire. A housekeeper would serve cocoa and chocolate-covered digestive biscuits, which Kelly used to wolf. The conversations ranged widely. He was, I now think, a parson with doubts about Christianity. He had a vision of society entirely new to me. He may not have been an original thinker but his educated and disciplined conscience opened many doors, and influenced my general attitudes. Eventually he left the church and the neighbourhood, and we no more went to All Hallows church hall.

Our meetings with the other troops came to an end when we moved to the *Discovery*. More than the move was involved. Our small group within the troop assumed an identity of its own. Possibly it was part of the process of growing up. We had all begun to work, and had some money and ideas of our own. We also had a project which dominated our lives for more than a year. We had long wanted a boat of our own, but of course had no hope of raising sufficient money. The opportunity came when we heard that a boat had been left behind at Blackwall when the *Discovery* was taken upriver to her permanent moorings at the Embankment. One Saturday morning, bearing a letter from Mr Thomas, we cycled down to investigate. She was a large Norwegian pram, a flat-bottomed boat with a long sloping bow designed for easy towing or pulling over ice. She was beautifully built of teak, and was about 15 feet long. The main timbers, as we were to discover with dismay afterwards, were stout enough for a seventy-four. The fittings were of gun metal, and copper air-tight tanks for buoyancy were mounted under the thwarts. She was in a very dilapidated condition from lying on a hard too long, but was structurally sound. We returned full of enthusiasm, the obliging Mr Thomas conducted the necessary negotiations, and on another Saturday morning we went down to take delivery.

This time we travelled by tram carrying a couple of oars. They were long and the conductor objected, but with Kelly's blarney we got on board almost decapitating the conductor in the process. There was another row when an inspector boarded the tram near the West India Dock, but by then Kelly had the other passengers on our side and he was told to *Git orf 'is bleeding 'igh 'orse*. He compromised by charging for the oars as luggage. It was almost knocking-off time when we got to the boat, and the craneman was anxious to get off. The pram had already been rigged for slinging, and as soon as we arrived the impatient craneman picked her up and lowered her into the water. We scrambled down a slimy wooden ladder let into the dock wall, and unbolted the sling. It disappeared from view and the crane trundled off before we realized that the boat was down to her gunwales in the water. The months of standing on a hard had shrunken her timbers, and only the air-tight tanks kept her afloat—barely. It was a tricky situation, but the dock was deserted and the incoming tide was well underway. We decided to chance the trip upriver although we could not sit down for water. Standing on the thwarts, and using one oar as a tiller, we slowly floated upstream.

From the shore it must have looked as if we were standing or walking on the water. *Like so many Jesus Christs*, said somebody. Only the gunwales were to be seen as the boat drifted sluggishly under water. We had been looking forward to an excursion and had come with the makings of a picnic, a bottle of cold tea and cheese and jam sandwiches. This we consumed standing. *Standing room only in the one and threes*, shouted Kelly, and there was general hilarity. Fortunately the river was almost deserted. Not even a coalboat passed to or from the upriver power stations. We drifted on in a giggly mood, waving to the few people to be seen on the banks and without mishap until we reached Tower Bridge. There we rammed one of the piers in spite of much pulling at the stern oar, gently but enough to topple most of us into the watery interior of the boat. A commotion could be heard from the bridge above, which was lined with the gaping heads of Saturday-afternoon promenaders. Somebody threw a life-belt, a lethal weapon if it had hit one of us but it fell with a splash into the river and floated upstream out of view. A river police launch came along and stood off from us, its engine turning slowly astern.

We knew the crew, and they knew that we were experienced watermen. A good deal of laughing and gesticulating followed as we tried to get away from the pier. It acted like a magnet, and with our bow apparently glued to it we bumped our way through a half circle until we came to rest in the dead water behind. Slowly, almost imperceptibly, we began to drift up-river again, this time stern first. It was ridiculous, and our giggles became uncontrollable as Tower Gardens and the Customs House went slowly by. London Bridge began to loom when the police launch circled again and the friendly sergeant coxswain threw us a line. We were gently pulled round until our bow was pointing upriver again. Then disaster almost struck when the launch increased speed. The sergeant had intended to tow us, but as soon as the line tautened and the pram got under way her bow went right under water. Another commotion followed as we all collapsed again into the now disappearing boat. Fortunately the man in the bow had only taken a turn round the forward thwart. He immediately released the line and the pram, like a clumsy gambolling whale, slowly righted itself. From then on the police launch stood off, and we drifted on bumping into some bridge piers until the Blackfriars bridges were safely cleared and the *Discovery* came into view. By sheer luck our arrival was beautifully timed. The tide had run its course and slackened as we approached the moorings. We tied up without help, but if we had been a few minutes late we would have drifted helplessly downriver again with the falling tide.

Later we lifted her on to the deck of the *Discovery*, caulked her and varnished her inside and out. She was a beautiful boat, but no sailer. She had no centreboard, and the price of fitting one was beyond us. Reluctantly we decided that she would have to be a powerboat, and that winter Rodgers heard of a car engine we could have for nothing. All we had to do was remove it from a car standing in a warehouse somewhere behind New Oxford Street. The warehouse was used to store props rented to theatres and film studios. The car was an old one and we were given the engine on condition it was removed before a certain day.

It was not easy, as any reader who has tried to remove an engine must know. We were not trained mechanics and had few tools. Nevertheless, all the bolts were removed after struggling for two or three nights with an inadequate inspection lamp and bleeding knuckles. Then came the major problem. We could borrow a block and tackle from the *Discovery*, but had no idea how to get the engine down to the ship. This was resolved by Kelly who arranged to hire a wheelbarrow for three old pennies from a yard behind the Elephant and Castle.

One bright and cold Saturday morning we met him at the Elephant Underground and collected the barrow from under one of the arches of the Southern Electric line. It was a typical costermonger's barrow, two wheels towards the front and two legs and a couple of stout handles at the rear. The carved frame was painted a faded blue, and at one side was a plate with the owner's name and a licence number. Rather selfconsciously we pushed it over Waterloo bridge to the warehouse with Kelly occasionally shouting *Penny a pound pears* and *Lovely toffee apples*. We had no difficulty in lifting the engine with the tackle and, after pushing back the gutted car, lowered it gently on to the barrow. Then we moved off, more slowly this time because of the weight. The traffic in New Oxford Street in those days was not one-way and we turned left then moved out to the middle of the road to turn right into Kingsway. The traffic lights were green but changed as we hurried forward to cross. An impatient Ford V8 moved out from Southampton Row. We tried to stop, but the momentum of the heavy engine was too much. The barrow came down slidingly on its legs, which cracked and bent as the weight continued to move forward. We came to a halt in the middle of the intersection, the engine still on the barrow but with the gearbox resting on the roadway between the handles.

The traffic was not thick, and a cab driver dismounted to survey the damage. He was young, and responded to Kelly who by this time was shouting, *Any old iron*. He beckoned to some passers-by, the barrow was righted and pushed into the left-hand kerb of Kingsway. We were grateful, but our predicament was still serious. We had to balance two or three hundredweight of metal on two wheels and move it about 1,000 yards, much of it downhill and with two tricky corners to navigate. The cabby gave us a short length of frayed rope from his trunk, and with two of us belaying on it from behind we moved slowly forward to the cheers of the assembled crowd. Some followed, and one or two helped until we reached the Aldwych with its swirling one-way

traffic jockeying for different lanes, when perhaps not unnaturally we were abandoned to our own devices. All went
well at first. We turned left towards the Law Courts, again
moving out to the middle of the road to turn right across the
Strand when we had passed Australia House. We aimed at
St Clement Danes and the unused stretch of road where
motorcycles can now be parked. Here we rested before
attempting the descent to the Embankment. It was to prove
our last and most dreadful mistake.

There was a lull in the traffic when we rested, but when
we moved forward again a Royal Mail van came round the
church from Fleet Street. It was travelling fairly fast, and
accelerating as do most drivers knowing that they are
approaching the broad plain of the beginning of the Strand
after the narrow ravine of Fleet Street. We hurried forward
to avoid it, and were moving at a sharp walking pace when
we reached what we thought was the safety of Arundel
Street. Alas, in the excitement we had forgotten that this
little cross street has a gradient of about one in seven, and
the barrow with its heavy load immediately charged forward
like a juggernaut. We managed to steady it a little by steering
into the gutter every few yards, but by the time we reached
Temple Place we were unstoppable. We swept into the
second one-way crescent at a smart running pace, then had
to swerve to the right to miss the usual line of parked cars
outside the Cable and Wireless building. Fortunately again,
there was no traffic and the slope to the river was less
precipitous. We slowed the barrow a little but could not
stop it. We could hear the traffic moving along the Embankment round the next corner, and final disaster seemed
inevitable. But as our mother used to say, *God is good*. He was
that afternoon. As we swerved again round the corner of
Embankment Gardens, past the spot where the down-and-

outs lined up for food and drink from the Silver Lady van, the traffic lights turned green. We were pulled, but at a slackening pace, across the main road and on to the tram lines which then ran on the river side of the Embankment.

We finally stopped opposite the steps to the *Discovery*. A tram was approaching, but we knew that it had to stop in spite of its clanging bell. It did, and with a final effort we pulled the barrow on to the pavement. We had made it, if only just. The damage, apart from our nervous systems, was two splintered barrow legs and a wheel loosened by the repeated steering into the gutter of Arundel Street. This took a lot of explaining when Kelly and some others returned the barrow, and ten bob for repairs. But it was worth it. We had delivered the engine safe and sound, at least to the side of the *Discovery*. The two naval pensioners were so impressed that without much grumbling they rigged up a tackle to lower the engine into the pram. We had already built the mountings in the stern, and with not too much trouble the engine was safely lowered to its final resting place. We secured it temporarily with four-inch nails until we could drill and position the bolts.

We had still not finished. The sternpost had to be bored for the propellor shaft, which meant that the pram had to be taken out of the water. We could not do this at the *Discovery*, and somebody, I have forgotten whom, found a mooring above Isleworth where we could pull her out of the water. We rowed her upstream, this time tight and dry, with pride. She was a handsome boat, and as we laboured on her weekend after weekend we attracted some handsome girls. I am afraid that we were corrupted, and not only by girls. The ones in Greenhithe were much easier. But for the first time we realized that if Benfleet was the arsehole of the Thames, sixty miles up it was rather pleasant. The river was narrow, not a real river any more although still tidal, but the banks were lush and alive. The small boats there were hardly serious craft but they were trim and neat. Instead of the isolation hospital on Long Reach we had riverside pubs, the towpath and pleasant houses. The drab greens and greys of the Essex marshes gave way to red tile and bright paint. Alas the enormous sky was lost. The upriver horizon was near, but the trees and general surroundings were postcard pretty. The girls did not lower their drawers as promptly as the bints in Greenhithe, but they seemed to be more desirable. I am not certain why. A few years later I would have regarded the Greenhithe girls as—more interesting? Certainly they were more basic. The girls we met above Isleworth were lower-middle class from nearby semis, and new to us. I suppose that is why they were so attractive. They reflected or observed a set of social and sexual standards which were somehow reassuring. Different as they were from the girls in Greenhithe, they were what I had been brought up to expect and respect.

The consequences were no doubt inevitable. Our tight little group became fissiparous. We continued to work on the pram, but the teak hardness of her sternpost was not the only reason why progress was slow. The final stages have slipped my memory. We eventually bored through the sternpost and mounted the propellor shaft. I can remember helping to fit the propellor, which had a ten-inch thrust, and which I had bought in a yachting store near the Minories. That I can remember clearly because I had looked at its display windows a hundred or more times walking from home to *The Times* or the *Discovery*. It was filled with Admiralty charts, pennants, compasses and other yachting paraphernalia. For me it had long been the most exciting shop window in London, much more exciting than the art shop beyond the Bank with its reproductions of Russell Flint nudes. It had been a special joy for me to go inside and buy the propellor after a somewhat lengthy discussion about horse-power and thrust. But I can't remember launching the pram after her conversion. Our concerted effort, in many ways splendid, to have a boat of our own faded in the final stage.

Again I suppose it was part of the process of growing up. Girls were certainly part of it, although I can't remember any of them clearly. Years later, on leave from Washington. I can remember embarrassing a girl sitting opposite me in an Underground train. Apparently I had been staring at her, and she suddenly got up and stood by the door. I was almost as embarrassed, but Isleworth came back suddenly in sharp focus. She could not have been one of the girls I knew, she was years younger, but the profile and hair, both rather heavy, were familiar. They reminded me, in the confused way memory has, of Schmidt's in Charlotte Street. I had taken that girl, or rather her spitting image, to the German restaurant before or after going to Sadlers Wells. I remembered that the opera had been Beethoven's *Fidelio*. That is why I had gone to Schmidt's and not to an Italian or French restaurant. The Wells and the Old Vic were also part of my growing up and growing away from the 2nd City of London Sea Scouts. Unlike sailing or rowing a boat, music or the theatre was intensely personal.

Then there was politics. For all our closeness and the amount of time we spent together, we rarely talked politics. Kelly was probably most responsible. The poorest of us, he never assumed that life could be improved by concerted or organized action. His Cockney humour was sharper, or more savage than ours, possibly because he always saw himself and his own in unequal contest with the world beyond. His humour was self-protective, for himself, his family and all East Londoners, if not all the poor. Believing that nothing would change, our mother would say that he made the best of it. For me, Kelly summed up the best and worst of Cockney life; the fortitude, the humour and sticking-together, and the basic pessimism and rejection of ambition. I liked him immensely, but his impatience with my perhaps naive political talk was bruising. My interest also continued to grow, fed with newspaper reports from Germany and eventually Spain and made exiting by local resistance to home-grown fascist bullyboys. I became a convinced socialist, and flirted with the communists only in part because they attracted interesting if not especially pretty girls.

Finally I was learning to write, or so I thought. I was determined to write once it was established that I could not be a merchant navy apprentice, first because of the lack of money and our mother's determination to get me into the print, and finally because my eyesight was not good enough. My ambition dovetailed neatly with our mother's intention, although she had no idea of this. She still saw me as a printer or a compositor, but for me writing meant writing for newspapers. It began with the *Red Duster*, which I wrote, edited, printed and published at irregular intervals at Crutched Friars and on the *Discovery*. It was a four-page quarto sheet printed in two colours. That is the red duster, or red ensign, was drawn in red on the masthead. Not a copy has survived, which is perhaps just as well. It could not have been very good. It was published for no other purpose than that I wanted to write and publish.

I did not seek contributions. I would have resented sharing the limited space with others. It was all my own work. The first page was devoted to news such as reports on our weekend activities, forthcoming events and rather snide accounts of the joint troop meeting at All Hallows church hall. Some of them must have been libellous. The inside pages carried articles about sailing boats and equipment, I'm afraid largely cribbed from the *Yachting World*, and a feature article. This was supposed to have been modelled on Robert Lynd's Saturday essay in the *News Chronicle*. I can remember one appalling piece about country pubs in which I said that men drank not for the sake of drinking but for good fellowship. The back page was supposed to be useful for those readers who wanted to pass the various scout tests for camping, cooking, splicing and what have you. Again it was largely a crib, this time from scout manuals, but I suppose it served the useful purpose of making information readily available. On reflection, I must have unwittingly pioneered the popularizing Sunday colour magazines. This interest, or passion, led me to Goldsmiths' College in New Cross where I attended evening classes on the art of writing. One of my first efforts, on sea scouting, was published by *The Times House Journal*, a monthly which was circulated among the staff of the paper. Another piece, believe it or not, was on the art of writing. Thus I drifted away from the 2nd City of London. Then the war came and I never saw any of them again.

# 6

ONE DAY in the autumn of 1934 our mother got a letter from Mr Hoar, the company secretary of *The Times*. He had a vacancy for a messenger and would she bring me for an interview the following Saturday at eleven. We arrived early, our mother always did, and were shown into a waiting room. It was heavily and well-furnished in mahogany, much better than the office in the new building which I used years later as deputy editor. We must have waited about fifteen minutes, during which time our mother inspected me and told me to speak up when spoken to. I don't remember being nervous. I had long assumed that I would work for *The Times*, and I knew parts of the building quite well because of the Christmas parties for the widows and orphans. Then we went in through the back door in Printing House Square which led to the mechanical departments and the staff restaurant. Even on a Saturday afternoon when no paper was to be published that night the place had for me a tension of hushed excitement. The back door was never closed, and was manned day and night, weekdays, weekends and holidays. One of the myths of Printing House Square, or P.H.S. as the building was known to the staff, was that a man used to sit at the back door every night with a large gladstone bag chained to his wrist. This went on for decades until one day Northcliffe, who then owned the paper, asked who he was. He was a clerk from Coutts Bank who, with his predecessors before him, had sat there every night with 200 gold sovereigns just in case a correspondent had to leave for foreign parts in a hurry after banking hours. Their vigil had begun after one night during the Napoleonic wars when a correspondent lost a Channel packet and a good story for the want of a few sovereigns.

Myth or not, I always felt that it could, indeed should have been true. The back door was that kind of place, I suppose because of the proximity of the mechanical departments which for me then were the heart of the paper. The staircase leading up to the mechanical departments was quite grand, with broad shallow steps and elegant curves round a broad well. Under it a discreet door led to the Private House, the original residence of the founder, John Walter I, which then housed the boardroom, the proprietors' offices, the editorial mess, and a couple of bedrooms, one of which was used by the reporter on weekend duty. As I recall, the weekend turn was from 4 p.m. Saturday until midday Sunday. Junior reporters were paid 25 shillings and were given a free day for what was a very cushy job. From time to time the man at the back door would bring in telegrams and Reuter tape, which more often than not could be left for the news room staffs when they came in on Sunday afternoon. About eight in the evening a manservant from the chief proprietor's house in Carlton House Terrace would serve dinner, a mixed grill or steak with half a bottle of claret and cheese and fruit to follow. He also served breakfast with the Sunday papers about nine in the morning. One manservant, long since retired and well into his eighties, still helped at the time of writing to serve luncheons in the boardroom.

Those weekend turns were of course well into the future, but when I was a boy we were allowed to peep into the panelled hall and boardroom with its portraits of the various Walters and an early Victorian painting entitled *Waiting for*

*The Times* showing a man with a carafe of madeira waiting impatiently for another to finish reading the paper. We would then ascend the low steps, past the door leading to the publishing or packing department, to a broad landing with a long noticeboard covered with announcements from the various sporting and social clubs, and to the right the swing doors leading to the composing room. It would be silent and dark on those Saturday afternoons, but peering through the heavy glass I could see the rows of type cases and beyond the linotype machines. We would mount the stairs to the next landing and the restaurant. Above were the reading room, the circulation department and a mysterious office labelled the *Marked Paper Dept*. All this is still fixed in my mind, although after joining the paper I was away for 30 years, first in the army and then abroad as a foreign correspondent, and the old building was torn down long before I returned from Washington.

It was in my mind while we waited that Saturday morning, until we were shown up to the third and top floor where the manager and such people had their offices. The old front building had a much narrower staircase than at the back, and the lift installed in the well could only carry three people. I can remember reading a notice below the control panel stating that messengers must not use the lift unless accompanying visitors. It was followed by a threat of instant dismissal. The lift moved so slowly that I had a good look down each descending corridor: the first with the editor's office, the home and foreign sub-editors' rooms, the editorial conference room and room 3 with its news agency tele-printers; the second with its offices for the foreign and home news editors, leader writers and specialists. My brother had earlier described this to me, which with my Christmas visits to the restaurant and the back building and our mother's assumption for our future led me to believe that P.H.S. was as much ordained for me as a public school, university college and London club are ordained for others in what may be described as more fortunate circumstances. The belief was reinforced by the interview with Mr Hoar. He was a plumpish and kindly man with a mouthful of teeth, and he might easily have been a headmaster welcoming Heren minor, the second or third generation of the family coming up to the old school. Except that our mother tried to do much of the talking.

It was a great moment for her. At last I was going into the print. I was claiming my birthright. She was finally doing her duty to her third and youngest child. But it wasn't all that good. I was aware of that, even though in those days of mass unemployment in Shadwell *The Times* offered some kind of opportunity. Mr Hoar said that I was to be a front door messenger. I was to be paid 17s. 6d. a week for the first probationary month, and then £1 a week with an annual two weeks holiday. There were to be annual rises, to £1. 7s. 6d. and then £1. 15s. od. a week. After that the pay would depend upon the department I went into. The possibility of my getting an apprenticeship was clearly remote. Mr Hoar did not say as much, but answered our mother defensively. She knew that they were given only to sons of fathers already in the trade, but mine had been dead too long for any real hope of preferment. What I did not know of at the time was the possibility of remaining a messenger for all of my working life. All the editorial messengers who worked at night were men, but Mr Hoar assured our mother that I should do well if I worked hard, behaved myself and went to night school. I could become a printer's reader or join one of the clerical departments. The possibility of becoming a reporter was never mentioned.

Our mother persisted. She was proud that our father was a journeyman rotary printer, and had kept his indenture certificate in a black tin box with her marriage lines and our birth certificates. It said that he was to serve his master for seven years, and 'he shall not commit fornication nor contract matrimony during the said term. He shall not play cards, dice, tables, or any unlawful games . . . haunt taverns, or playhouses, nor absent himself from his said master's service day or night unlawfully'. She was much taken by the language, as she was by the fact that shop stewards in print unions are known as fathers of the chapel. She saw a direct connection with the medieval church which somehow raised even higher the status of the printing trades. She had brought his indentures along that morning, but received no promises or encouragement. Mr Hoar was in no position to give either. The unions decided who was to be apprenticed. This was brought home to me soon afterwards. One of the other boys at the front door—I think his name was Roberts—was the son of the assistant printer, or the second-in-command in the composing room. He was always rather smug because he knew that he was guaranteed an apprenticeship. To rub it in, he even looked like his father. Although only fifteen or sixteen years old, his heavy face and body were a junior version of the assistant printer. But on that Saturday morning Mr Hoar could only say that I was to begin work a week later. Which I did, at 8.30 a.m., and wearing my best, or rather only suit.

There was little trouble at school, certainly no formal objections. The headmaster was accustomed to boys in my year suddenly disappearing. He might have regretted or even welcomed my departure. I had no indication. But Mr Miller and Miss Nixon were sorry to see me go. I was then a firm disciple, or *chela*, to Miss Nixon. I accepted her judgements on literature unquestioningly. I'm not so certain about Mr

Miller. He was an older and more experienced man. I suppose that he knew that students—what a posh word in our circumstances—had to leave school for all kind of economic and social reasons. All I know is that I regretted leaving him. For me, that sun-tanned face, with its hooked nose and light blue eyes, rising above the winged collar and brown tweed suit, was about as close as I ever got to a father. I gloried in what appeared to be his irrepressible enthusiasm for ideas and knowledge. If he was around today I would do my best to hire him as a senior leader writer. In any event, I left school the following Friday without any indication that my departure was of any importance.

So much for the old *alma mater*. Otherwise the transition from school to *The Times* was easy enough. The work was not exactly demanding, and at least I had a bit of money in my pocket. Not much. After the first probationary month, a few coppers were deducted from my £1 a week for whatever it was before National Health. My fares were 8d. a day, or 3s. 4d. a week. Our mother allowed me 9d. a day for lunch, or 3s. 9d a week. Thus the overheads, if that is the word, were 7s. 1d. a week. Of the remainder I gave our mother 7s. 6d. a week, which left me with about five shillings a week. In fact, I had rather more. Instead of catching the train from Shadwell Underground to Blackfriars, I would walk to the Minories station and thus halve the fare to 2d. In the evening I would go home on a No. 15 bus which cost only tuppence. Thus my five shillings a week was increased to 6s. 8d. Then I would add to it by economizing on my lunch, of which more later. But those few silver and copper pieces in my pocket made all the difference. They opened a new world to me, of which again more later.

As to the work, four boys were employed at the front door under the command of the chief commissionaire, a Mr

McCluskie. He was certainly in command. On the whole, he was a nice man, who could laugh at a joke, but he had a tight Northern Irish face topped with tighter ginger curly hair and the discipline he imposed was no less tight. Without actually lining us up on parade, he inspected us each morning for neatness, telling one to shine his shoes better on the morrow and another to get a haircut. Neckties were obligatory, as was a general respectful demeanour. This training served me well when I joined the army during the second world war, especially when I went to Sandhurst. The Royal Military Academy was then reduced to a tank officers' training school, but the old habits were continued by the staff. We were always addressed as Gentlemen Cadets, but discipline was stricter than in fighting regiments. Some found it irksome, but with the cadets from superior public schools I accepted it as normal because of Mr McCluskie.

In the morning, after inspection, we sorted and distributed letters to the various departments. The building was divided into four delivery and collection routes, which we pursued every 20 minutes. In between we conducted visitors to and from offices—nobody was allowed to enter the building unaccompanied. Again this mindless task was educational. As I have already observed, English society in those days was deferential. The staff was rigidly divided into three large groups, editorial, mechanical and management with its large retinue of clerks and secretaries. Some of these assumed the distantness of their superiors, who were often very imperious. The manager, Mr Lints Smith, was a kind of English pope, and his secretary a member of the college of cardinals. We were divided not only by the jobs we were paid to do but also by the classes to which we were assumed to belong. The senior commercial men and their secretaries could be very demanding, and rather nasty.

One advertising manager wore a winged collar, a cravat with a pearl tiepin, black jacket and waistcoat and striped trousers. He always had an impatient look, as if he was deeply concerned with affairs of state, and would look over and through me when I entered his office every 20 minutes with my little tray of letters. His nostrils would twitch as if I smelled. His secretary was no less imperious. She was a middle-aged woman, plumpish with her black hair done up in a bun. She always looked angry. I suppose a psychiatrist could have explained her condition. Whatever it was, my meekish appearance generally aroused what can only be explained as aggressive tendencies. She had a loud, high-pitched voice, which I afterwards heard on the stage and then much later in clubs and plantation bungalows in British colonial territories. On at least one occasion she shouted at me for some alleged stupidity. Then there was an accountant who was always nasty. We were taught to tap on doors before entering offices and he would look up expectantly. He also wore a black jacket and waistcoat with striped pants but a turned-down stiff collar over what I suppose was a school or club tie. He would look over his pince-nez and then growl when he saw that it was just me. It could not have been a personal dislike. I was only a messenger to be growled at or ignored. He behaved similarly with the other messengers, but the dislike became intensely personal after the war when I was transferred from the reporters' room to the foreign side. In those days—I am now writing of the early post-war years—there was nobody in the office to buy air tickets and make other arrangements. Foreign correspondents were gentlemen, and were assumed to prefer to make their own arrangements and charge the paper afterwards. This did not surprise me. During the war I was attached to the Indian Army whose officers were also gentlemen and expected to make their own arrangements. I actually paid my rail fare from Poona to Burma, and claimed it afterwards. The possibility that I might have been killed in action before the pay office in Meerut got around to paying me may have been a factor, but there was also a small advantage for the officer. He went first class for the price of a second class ticket, and was eventually awarded the cost of a first class fare. No such perks were built into the system in P.H.S. You just paid your way and claimed later. It had a wonderful, almost awesome simplicity, permitting one of the world's largest and most comprehensive news services to be run by a foreign news editor, a young assistant and a secretary.

But it was also a gentlemanly system. When the decision was made to translate me from the home to the foreign side, I received a short memorandum from the foreign news editor, Mr Ralph Deakin. It said: *The Foreign News Editor presents his compliments and looks forward to meeting Mr Heren at his early convenience.* I answered in a similarly oblique manner, and was eventually received one Monday morning. Mr Deakin had an unlined, plumpish face and a tight control over his lips. His preciseness of speech and manner was razor sharp. He sat upright behind his desk wearing a grey alpaca jacket. Behind him his bowler hat rested on a small shelf, which must have been made for that purpose. I did not know what to expect, but I was excited and assumed that he would also recognize what a great moment it was for me. I was also departing for a fairly dangerous assignment and anticipated a little drama. The conversation went something like this:

*Mr Heren?*

*Mr Deakin?*

*Good morning.*

*Good morning, sir.* (I had been a senior subaltern too long not to address an officer of field rank otherwise.)

*I understand that you want to go overseas for us.*

*Yessir.*

*When do you think you could go?*

*Before the end of the week.*

*Come now. We don't have to be too precipitate. Surely you need time to wind up your affairs.* (I was recently out of the army and had no affairs whatsoever, and very little else. I said so. There was quite a lengthy pause, and then)

*It is rather strange I think, Mr Heren. It takes only ten or fifteen minutes to appoint a foreign correspondent of The Times, and yet it can take twenty years to get rid of him.*

He went on to say that he confidently expected a long and fruitful partnership, but made no mention of the assignment, what was expected of me, or when and how I was to get to India. Eventually I asked where I could get the air ticket. He looked at me, lips pursed and eyebrows raised, and said:

*Try Thomas Cooks.*

I did, and not unnaturally they wanted to know about payment. Eventually I went to the accountant, and explained that I had been appointed as a foreign correspondent and needed X number of pounds to buy a ticket to India. He fell into a curious rage, apparently resenting that I had now joined the gentlemen. Only with the greatest reluctance did he finally authorize payment, but holding me responsible for the fact that in those days airliners did not have an economy class or steerage. The resentment persisted for a number of years. When I was in Palestine covering the birth of Israel and the first war with the Arabs he insisted that I send weekly expense accounts although at the time the postal service with Britain was disrupted. The final attack came when I was South-east Asia correspondent based on Singapore. It was a wonderful job, if exhausting and occasionally dangerous. My parish included Malaya, Thailand, Indo-China, Indonesia and the Borneo territories. This was the period when the French were fighting the Vietminh in Indo-China, the British were prosecuting what they called the emergency in Malaya, Indonesia was suffering under the megalomania of Sokarno and Thailand had *coups* every three or four months. I was travelling much of the time, and just might have got my expenses wrong. I doubt it. Working for *The Times* in those days made one penny-conscious, but one day I got a letter from the accountant. He regretted that I had a deficit of £68. 10s. 5d. and that I had ignored earlier letters, and had directed that this sum be deducted from my salary.

I had not received an earlier notification of this foul crime, no proof was provided, and of course no mention was made of the fact that I had been risking my neck in little but vicious wars for some time. In those days *The Times*, as I was once told by Mr Deakin, was not interested in the adventures of its correspondents. That I had been doing a reasonably good job in a very newsworthy area for a salary much less than that of a home reporter on the *Daily Mirror* was also ignored. I also received the letter after return from a rather trying time in Indo-China, and I answered in a towering rage. I would sue the company and the accountant under the Truck Acts if he as much as deducted a farthing from my farcical salary. Eventually I got letters from the editor and manager saying that it was all a mistake, that I was highly appreciated, and that if I owed the company anything it would be written off because of my fine services, etc, etc, etc.

These incidents were typical of the then management, but I digress. Back in the thirties when I was still a messenger, middle-class snobbery and such class resentments were not found elsewhere in the building. The senior editorial staff were always polite. It might have been an officer-and-man relationship, but was still civilized. Of course, the senior editorial men were treated as officers, and the Editor with respect normally reserved for the C.I.G.S. Every morning, between eleven and twelve, one of us would stand on the steps outside looking for his Rolls-Royce. When it was seen approaching from the Embankment the chief commissionaire would be signalled. He would ring down the lift and a second boy would hold the gate open. The boy out front would open one of the swing doors and say, *Good morning*, *sir*, the commissionaire would open the door leading to the lift, and salute, and the second boy would close the lift gates with an ejaculated *Sir*. For a year or more I was often the first or second boy, and still have a memory of Mr Geoffrey Dawson. He invariably wore a double-breasted flannel or serge suit and a homburg, except on Monday mornings when he returned from a country-house weekend wearing a tweed suit. He carried a stick or umbrella, with which he saluted us as he hurried past. Always he seemed in a hurry, but his good manners may have required this to avoid or reduce obvious displays of the power and the glory of his office. Mr Barrington-Ward, the assistant editor, would arrive about the same time. We were not required to open the door for him, but the commissionaire generally rang down the lift. He was the more intense man, and wore darker suits. His face was pallid but alive. He always thanked the messengers for any service done although he seemed constantly preoccupied.

In spite of these divisions, the class antagonisms between the managerial and the lesser breeds and the polite superiority of the senior editorial people, everybody who worked for *The Times* was supposed to be a member of one big happy family known as the Companionship. Somehow anybody and everybody, from messengers, charladies and clerks to compositors, managers and editors, was joined in a mystical union dedicated to producing *The Times*. Working for the paper, no matter our accent, station or job, we were assumed to be removed from ordinary industrial strife. We were not employees or hands, but Companions. The metaphysics are difficult to explain. I can only compare the Companionship with the English army at Agincourt under Henry the Fifth. Now a young reporter working in P.H.S. would only giggle. The comparison would be too far fetched. If I was thirty years younger my giggles would be uncontrollable because looking back the appearances of the Companionship were both feudal and old-fashioned. The Chief Companion, the late Lord Astor of Hever, who was then Major J. J. Astor, was the manorial lord who actually lived in a castle. He looked the part: tall, thin, and with a distinguished limp because of the leg he lost in the first world war. His face would be instantly recognized on any cinema screen or television late, late movie, as that of a British army officer with its small regular features with a close-cropped moustache. Moreover, he took his manorial duties very seriously. The Hever Days, mentioned in an early chapter, were only the highlight of the Companionship's crowded social calendar, in which he played an active part. The lady of the manor, Lady Violet, also looked and played her part. She must have been very beautiful when young, and when I first saw her she had those soft chocolate-box looks which went so well with the floppy big hats she always seemed to wear. It was established that she loved her garden at Hever so much that she rarely came to London, but she was always present at the summer show of *The Times* Horticultural Society, accompanied by her head gardener—a Scotsman of course—who would support her expert judging.

The giggle threshold was therefore low, at least in retrospect. Major Astor may have taken his duties over-seriously because of his American background—he was, as it were, only a second-generation Englishman—but he was an extra-ordinarily modest man. His arrivals and departures at P.H.S. had none of the pomp which attended the movements of the Editor. This may have been because his Rolls cars—he had a splendid open tourer as well as the normal town car or cars—always went to the back door instead of the front. There the door keeper and messengers had none of the refined politeness of the front door. His chauffeur would open the door and he would disappear quickly into the Private House. But apart from the architecture of P.H.S. and the differences between the front and back door staffs, he was also a shy man as I first discovered when as a messenger I held some interior door open for him. He hurried forward in spite of the discomfort of his artificial leg and thanked me profusely.

Again years afterwards, when I was home on leave from my South-east Asian assignment, I was invited to some social function at his house in Carlton House Terrace. I was asked to come early because the Colonel—he had meanwhile been promoted to command the Fleet Street Home Guard during the second world war—wanted a few words with me. I was shown into a room or gallery hung with tapestries, but my somewhat vulgar attention was attracted to the ceiling which had recently been redone with a great deal of gold leaf. The time was comparatively soon after the war. It was winter and cold outside, at least for a man who had spent his few adult years east of Suez. Outside London still looked war-worn and tatty. Some kind of rationing was still in force. Against this background of cold austerity the ceiling was ostentatious in its glory. The colonel came in, and perhaps because the tipple that night was to be champagne he gave me and himself a couple of fingers of malt whisky and then asked about my adventures. Modesty not being one of my weaknesses I described some fully, but my eyes kept straying to that ceiling.

I was a good reporter in those days perhaps because I rarely hesitated to ask a pertinent question. Eventually I said how handsome the ceiling was and asked how much it cost. If he was startled by the question, he did not show any embarrassment. Instead, he said that after the years of war and the dreariness of rationing he had decided that some self-indulgence was permissible. It was a handsome room and the tapestries demanded to be set off. Well, to answer my question the refurbishing has cost £25,000. I must have gaped. I had not then served in the United States and there are limits to the knowingness of young foreign correspondents, but the Colonel gave me another whisky and asked if I was looking forward to returning to India. He may have been having me on but his manners were superb.

I am willing to entertain the proposition that manners make the man, but for P.H.S. the important thing about Major-Colonel-Lord Astor was that in spite of his other interests and investments—he was one of the wealthiest men in Britain and had vast holdings in the United States—he saw his first duty to *The Times*. It would have been very trying for a less modest or controlled man. He could declare open the annual show of the Camera Club, but the Editor alone was responsible for the contents of the paper. Even in those days the unions were too strong to be mucked about. He was a constitutional monarch rather than a manorial lord, and apparently content with the trappings instead of the substance of power. As with such monarchs, he was not altogether powerless. A painting hanging in the Blue Room at P.H.S. indicates his position. It portrays him sitting in his office and conversing with the Editor and Manager. Clearly he had an influence in a largish area not denied to him by the terms of the Editor's appointment and the power of the unions. I am told that his influence was generally for the good of the paper, although in his later years he was probably too cautious. Necessary changes such as putting news on the front page were delayed much too long because of his dedication to what he must have seen as a British institution rather than a newspaper which had to make a profit to survive. It did in fact make a profit most years, but only by working within strict editorial and financial boundaries. It was in danger of being left behind when control eventually passed to Lord Thomson.

As a messenger, I was of course aware only of the fringe benefits made possible by the Companionship. Physically these included a large sports ground at Ravensbourne in suburban Kent with a well-equipped clubhouse, a boathouse at Barnes for the Rowing Club, a gymnasium in the basement of P.H.S. with superb showers for the Boxing Club, a dark-room for the Camera Club and the Staff Restaurant. The sports and social clubs were many and varied, ranging from all the usual ball games, including golf, to music and dramatics. Their activities were reported every month in *The Times House Journal*. The forthcoming events in its October 1937 issue gives some indication of this activity.

DARTS LEAGUE (1936–37) FINAL AND DINNER
  Ravensbourne—Saturday, 16 October
SWIMMING CLUB ANNUAL GALA
  Marshall Street Baths—Saturday, 23 October
FOOTBALL CLUB SUPPER AND DANCE
  Ravensbourne—Saturday, 30 October
PRINTERS PENSION CORPORATION WHIST DRIVE
  Printing House Square—Saturday, 6 November
TENNIS CLUB DANCE
  Ravensbourne—6 November
DANCE AND CABARET AT THE WHARNCLIFFE ROOMS
  Saturday, 13 November

COUNTY HOCKEY MATCH, KENT V. SURREY
  Ravensbourne—Saturday, 20 November
BOXING CLUB TOURNAMENT
  Stadium Club—Thursday, 25 November
THE TIMES FOOTBALL CLUB DINNER AND DANCE
  Ravensbourne—Saturday, 27 November
BADMINTON CLUB DINNER AND DANCE
  Ravensbourne—Saturday, 4 December
MID-WEEK FOOTBALL CLUB DINNER AND DANCE
  Ravensbourne—Saturday, 11 December
INTERDEPARTMENTAL CRICKET LEAGUE DANCE
  Ravensbourne—Saturday, 1 January
MID-WEEK CRICKET CLUB SUPPER AND CONCERT
  Ravensbourne—Saturday, 8 January
THE TIMES FOOTBALL CLUB DANCE
  Ravensbourne—Saturday, 15 January
INTERDEPARTMENTAL CRICKET LEAGUE DINNER
  Ravensbourne—Saturday, 22 January
TENNIS CLUB DANCE
THE TIMES FOOTBALL CLUB DANCE
  Stationers' Hall—Saturday, 5 February
MUSICAL AND DRAMATIC SOCIETY
  Production of *The Arcadians*
  Guildhall School of Music Theatre
  10, 11, 12 February
THE TIMES CRICKET CLUB DANCE
  Ravensbourne—Saturday, 26 February
MID-WEEK CRICKET CLUB DINNER AND DANCE
  Ravensbourne—Saturday, 5 March
HOCKEY AND BADMINTON DANCE
  Ravensbourne—Saturday, 26 March
CAMERA CLUB DINNER
  Ravensbourne—Saturday, 2 April

Then followed various fixtures, announcements of a Camera Club competition and a meeting of the Christian Union and a request to make a note of these events to prevent clashing with other engagements.

This and other lists of events provided only the framework of what was almost a closed society. Many Companions chose to live in the Bromley area not only because of the all-night train service, which was essential for night workers, but also because they wanted to be near Ravensbourne sports ground. Hundreds of family lives were lived between the two poles of P.H.S. and Ravensbourne. Boys followed their fathers into P.H.S. where quite often they met their future wives. Their marriages were recorded in the *House Journal* as were their group activities, prowess on the sports field, and eventually their retirements and deaths. Every Companion was given an obituary. The files of the House Journal, bound in blue and embossed with gold provide the evidence. Here are a few excerpts:

#### WEDDINGS

The marriage of Mr R. J. Day, of the Accounts Dept., and Miss M. E. Kilbourn, of the Subscription Dept., took place at St George's Church, Bickley, on Saturday, 3 September. The Rev. W. Trevor Rees officiated at a most impressive ceremony and a large congregation testified to the popularity of the Bride and Bridegroom . . .

#### INTERDEPARTMENTAL DARTS LEAGUE: FINAL MATCH AND SUPPER

The final match was between the Engineers (winners of the Day Section) and the Night Messengers (winners of the Night Section) and the match resulted in a win for the former by two straight games. After the issue had been settled, both teams, together with numerous friends and supporters, sat down to enjoy a supper and concert which in every way was highly satisfying . . .

During the evening a musical programme was presented which proved a great success in every way. Miss E. H. Mecham, soprano, opened the programme with two numbers which were received with great applause and later in the evening her fine rendering of 'Cherry Ripe' and 'Stars in My Eyes' were greatly appreciated . . .

## SOME IMPRESSIONS OF THE WHARNCLIFFE CARNIVAL: AN EVENING OF REUNION AND REVELRY

There's no mistaking the mood of these annual gatherings at the famed Wharncliffe Rooms, another of which took place on Saturday, 13 November. From the moment the merrily-intentioned ones put foot over the threshold of one of London's most beautiful ballrooms, and, having discarded top-coats and 'toppers', assumed the motley for a few hectic hours, the show goes with a 'bang'! Or, perhaps, in these days of Duke Ellington and the 'Big Apple', it should read— the show goes on with a 'swing'! . . .

## WIDOWS AND ORPHANS CHRISTMAS PARTY

The Annual Party given by the Restaurant Committee to the Widows and Orphans of the Companionship took place on Saturday, 8 January. Evidence of an approaching festive occasion had been apparent in the Restaurant some days in advance when a huge Christmas tree, gaily decked out in shimmering ornaments and illuminated by multi-coloured lights made its appearance, to be followed by a wonderful collection of toys destined for the children. And what toys they were! Large dolls' houses, huge dolls, electrical and Meccano sets, and many other things which could not fail to bring joy to any child's heart. . . .

**THREE PACKED HOUSES FOR THE PRESENTATION OF
'THE ARCADIANS'**

The musical farce *The Arcadians*, produced by the Musical and Dramatic Society on the evenings of February 10, 11, and 12, was an undoubted success. Many who had not been privileged to see previous performances of the Society were surprised at its exceedingly fine presentation, while those who regularly follow its efforts were pleased that it has now set a new standard to maintain in its future productions. . .

**THE RAVENSBOURNE FETE: LETTERS OF APPRECIA-
TION FROM MAJOR AND LADY VIOLET ASTOR.**

*18, Carlton House Terrace, S.W.1.*
*July 7, 1938*

Dear Mr Kent,

It was a real surprise to receive from the Staffs of *The Times* and The Book Club last Saturday a Miniature of my daughter-in-law, and I cannot tell you how delighted I am with it. It is a very good likeness, with a most charming expression.

Will you convey to all my very sincere thanks for this Miniature, and, above all, for this expression of friendship which I so greatly value?

I must also thank you for the perfectly beautiful basket of flowers which was presented to me. They in themselves were a handsome present, so I feel that my friends at Ravensbourne have more than spoilt me.

I so enjoyed the Side-Shows and my ride in the 'Donkey Derby', and I shall value my Prize which my steed of 30 years won for me in such fine style!

Owing to the admirable arrangements at Ravensbourne, the atmosphere could not have been more enjoyable, and it is always a happiness to my husband and myself to share in the afternoon's fun. What a pity it was that the rain came down at the end of the proceedings!

With again my grateful thanks to you and to all who have so generously contributed towards the lovely Miniature of my daughter-in-law, which is a beautiful addition to my 'Gallery'.

Yours sincerely,<br>VIOLET ASTOR

## THE TIMES V. LORDS AND COMMONS
### HOME SIDE WIN BY SEVEN WICKETS

The groundsman had prepared a perfect wicket, and on winning the toss from Major Astor, Lord Ebbisham had no hesitation in deciding to bat. Twenty-eight runs had been added before the first wicket fell, and with Howard Wilkins and Lord Dunglass together, the score mounted steadily until. . . .

## UP THE BRIDAL PATH
### A SUBSCRIPTION DEPARTMENT SERIAL STORY

Readers of The House Journal will have missed during recent months the regular article featuring weddings in the Subscription Department, but this month we return with renewed vigour to report the surrender of two more of our number to the wiles of the opposite sex. Next month will also see a further instalment to this thrilling serial, provided, of course, that the hero and heroine are still in the same frame of mind.

### CHAPTER I

On 8 July members of the Subscription Department and a few friends met to witness a presentation to Mr Frank E. Webley. The banns of marriage had already been called three times, and it was getting perilously near the day.

Mr Gordon Brown, in asking Mr Webley to accept a canteen of cutlery as a wedding gift from his colleagues, reminded him. . . .

CHAPTER 2

Miss Hettie Putnam having spent nearly 15 years in the Stationery and Subscription Departments, and Mr Jack Evans having been a life member of the Subscription Department, it was felt that departmentally this wedding should be recorded as another Subscription victory.

Owing to the popularity of the bride, whose father and brother are respected members of the Staff, and of the bridegroom, who is honorary secretary of The Times Cricket Club, and also represents the Office in other branches of sport, it was only to be expected that there would be a number of presentations in the form of wedding gifts. . . .

OBITUARY: MR J. WOODHEAD

It is with deep regret that we have to record the death of Mr Jack Woodhead, which occurred on September 7 after a short illness. He had just reached his sixtieth year.

Woodhead was a warehouseman in the Sundry Publications Department for over twenty years, and, in spite of a modest and retiring disposition, his cheerful and willing ways caused him to be known and liked by a wide circle of friends. . . .

The editorial generally remained aloof, but this tight little world was open to all members of the staff, or Companions, including messengers. I never did much like ball games, but I was a member of the Camera Club and the Boxing Club. The latter was held in high esteem, perhaps because of the patronage of the Manager and certainly because of Pat Floyd, the winner of the Golden Gloves and many other trophies, who wore its colours. Two evenings a week I would go down to the gym and train under Alf Garrett, a tough lightweight who was given a job on the paper because of his boxing prowess. It was all very serious. We would skip and shadow box, and go for long runs along the Embankment. Much was expected of me at first. I was strongly built and nippy on my feet, but experience showed that I had one fatal weakness. My eyes would close every time I saw a straight right coming for my face. The weakness was recognized, and my training intensified. Some progress was thought to have been made, and I was entered in an amateur championship fought at the Stadium Club in Holborn. I shall never forget it.

The Stadium Club, destroyed in the second world war, was then known as the centre of amateur boxing in London. It was a shabby but serious place which attracted fans unconnected with amateur clubs. I have long since forgotten the differences between amateur and professional boxing, apart from money, except that the first was supposed not to be savage. We were supposed to be concerned with the niceties of the Noble Art rather than battering opponents insensible. The audience was required to remain silent. No shouting or applause was allowed until the end of the bout, which was disconcerting when my chance of glory came.

It was a cold night, outside and inside the hall, and all the colder because mine was one of the first fights of the evening. I did not have a dressing gown and came out of the changing room shivering in my gym vest and shorts. I was wearing plimsolls and not boxing boots. The hall seemed huge, and I was half defeated before clambering on to the brightly-lighted and silent ring. Defeat was made almost certain by the arrival of my opponent. He came loping down the aisle in a dressing gown of bright shiny stuff, recognizing and waving to his friends and supporters in the crowd. He swung lightly over the ropes, discarded his robe, and did some loosening-up exercises. He sanded his beautiful boots, held up his gloves for the seconds to inspect, and again waved to the crowd. All this time he had his back to me as I sat like a lump of chilled lard in my corner. Then suddenly he turned and I almost jumped out of the ring. He seemed all flowing muscle—I discovered afterwards that he was a railway fireman who spent his days shovelling a couple of tons of coal into the furnace of an express locomotive—without an ounce of superfluous flesh anywhere. His face had a frightening ferocity enhanced by the rubber teeth guards which a second fitted in his mouth. I did not hear what the referee said and seemed to lose the use of my eyes when the bell went. My seconds said something and I reluctantly moved forwards into a pink mist. It cleared and there was this dancing dervish prancing around me and making lightning jabs at my body. I tried to remember all that I had been taught, but it was no good. My eyes kept closing. I survived the first round, but not for long. After another minute of near-massacre my second threw in the towel.

This ended my dream of becoming a second Pat Floyd, but I remained a member of the Boxing Club for the exercise. And because of the baths. We had no bathroom at home, and I could hardly take a bath in a tin tub in front of the fire at my age. The public baths in St George's were always crowded, and a bit mean. In comparison the baths at *The Times* were sheer luxury. There were rows of them, showers and long baths, glistening with white tile and stainless steel taps and rails, and with an unending supply of hot water. I would wallow in them with the tap trickling hot water to maintain an almost unbearable heat. Our mother would warn me about catching cold, but I must have been the cleanest boy in Shadwell. The baths in the gym were further proof of the superiority of *The Times*, and of my good fortune in being a

Companion. Another was the Staff Restaurant, to which I brought a professional eye having lived above and behind a coffee shop all my life. Again the comparison was marked. *The City of Dublin Dining Rooms* was clean. The table tops were scrubbed, and the floor was swept and freshly sanded with sawdust every night. The high-backed settles might now have an old-world charm if they had survived the blitz, but the overall impression was of dim dinginess. The clientele was polite but hardly well-dressed. Their dockers' hooks scraped along the backs of the settles as they slid in and out of the stalls. Many drank tea from their saucers. Few ate with their mouths closed.

In contrast, the Staff Restaurant was, as the name implied, a real restaurant, and moreover was licensed to serve drinks. It looked attractive: large, light and airy, and the quality of the furnishings was superior to the average Soho restaurant. The many tables, seating four, were always covered with clean white tablecloths and decorated with fresh flowers. The waitresses wore a green uniform, with white caps and aprons. Women ate in a smaller room behind the cashier's desk, but not because the main dining room was rowdy. The noise rarely rose above a well-mannered hum. The canteen, as it was inevitably called, could have been mistaken for a middle-class restaurant in a county town such as Canterbury or Exeter. The food was no worse, and was cheaper as were the drinks. For instance, a whisky cost 8d., or less than 4p. The atmosphere changed as each day wore on. The rather genteel market-town atmosphere prevailed at lunch and teatime, but afterwards the tablecloths would disappear except in the section near the stage reserved for the editorial staff—mainly the subs, or sub-editors. It began to look more like a works canteen as overalls and aprons replaced the jackets of the commercial and clerical staffs. The smaller room, where the bar was, looked like a suburban pub instead of a suburban hen party, except no pub remained open so long—from midday until the early hours of the next morning—and few could have sold more drinks. The heavy drinkers from the foundry and machine room downed two or three pints each between editions. Sub-editors, many of whom were Scotsmen, stood at one end of the bar sipping whisky before retiring to their reserved section for supper.

Day and night the menu cards listed a choice of soup, three or four main dishes and as many afters. The average bill was about a shilling. Mine was a good deal less. I was well-fed at home and could afford to economize at lunchtime. Most days I would only have soup, which cost tuppence, and some kind of pudding for the same price. Custard cost a penny extra. Maud, the pleasant waitress at whose tables I sat, always gave me plenty of bread with the soup and an extra large helping of suet or bread pudding.

This was *The Times* Companionship, an extraordinary admixture of a country club, a town club and a tight social unit comparable to the tenants of a large estate belonging to a philanthropic squire. It was a bit spurious as most contrived organizations must be, but it worked. The staff were well taken care of in almost every possible way, not least in believing that they belonged to an exclusive group engaged in an honourable enterprise. It has all gone now, along with the old building and for that matter the life I knew in Shadwell. Some of the sporting clubs have survived, but the canteen is now nothing more than an industrial canteen, impersonal, self-service and damp formica. Perhaps it was a long time coming. As a social unit the Companionship reflected the manners and pretensions of a period long since gone. Major Astor was accepted in more ways than one. Clerks earning about £5 a week aspired to a version of his life style with its emphasis on sport and country pursuits. Social habits were also derivative. Ravensbourne was their Hurlingham, the Staff Restaurant their Reform or Garrick club, and the Wharncliffe nights their hunt balls. At such winter functions they always appeared in dinner jackets. One can giggle, but the Companionship was built on a solid rock, joint participation in the wonderful enterprise of publishing *The Times*. This has survived to some extent between the editorial and production staffs because few other jobs can be as satisfying and exciting. Few others can require personal effort and initiative on so many levels, or can be so constantly demanding. Other trades and occupations have their busy periods. Regiments can have their hours of glory, but newspaper publishing is a nightly drama played against the clock. And of course newspapers have no control over their basic raw material, news. It can break at any time, but editions must be produced within a rigid schedule. And except during strikes, more often than not called by unions not directly involved, the editorial and production men never fail each other.

I played no part in their exciting endeavour when I was a day messenger. The process of producing a paper was only beginning when I finished work at five, but after boxing in the gym and wallowing in one of those wonderful baths I would occasionally go back upstairs to watch. Then, as now, there was no place more exciting than the stone just before edition time. The columns of type were slid out of their galleys to make up a page, and late corrections had to be made and stories cut to fit. Many nights news came in late, and the page would have to be changed within minutes. It was at these heavy metal tables where the editorial and printing men met on equal terms. They worked together well, but each man only doing his own job. Even in the heat and excitement of getting away a late page the Night Editor or subs could not touch type. Years later, when I worked in the subs for a few weeks before going overseas, this strict division of labour infuriated and frustrated me, but of course the stonehands must have found an indecisive sub no less infuriating. I can remember one night when I was attached to the then Night Editor, Leslie Smith. He was an immensely calm man who looked as a classics don ought to look. He had long white hair and a thin brown face. He must have been born for the job. Nothing rattled him. He seemed to move about the office in a portable pool of calm. I doubt that his facial muscles had ever registered anger. His voice was always low and even. That night, a quiet night, he asked me if I would mind if he stayed longer at the club where he dined. Naturally I assented because I would be left in charge of the paper. The Editor had gone home. Some senior men were still working on the editorial floors, but I would be in charge at the front line. No page would be locked up and sent to the foundry without my nod. And if anything went wrong I would be solely responsible.

Things began to go wrong soon after Smith left for the Garrick or whatever his club was. A light above the Printer's desk blinked and I strolled nonchalantly across to answer the phone. It was one of the foreign subs, who said that the results of the Hungarian elections were coming through and would I make space for half a column on the bill page. It promised to be a long story, but half a column was probably all we could handle for the early edition. They were the last free elections to be held in Hungary. Not that I knew that then, but the paper was interested in eastern Europe in those immediate post war years and I did not question the sub's judgment. In those days we still had advertisements on the front and the bill page was the main news page opposite the leader page. A replaced story could not be thrown away because it had to be newsworthy to be on the bill page. I rejigged the page and wrote the headlines. All was going well when that light flashed again. It was the home subs this time. The first flashes were coming through on the attempt to get an abandoned ship in tow somewhere in the Atlantic. Time was getting on, but could I get a third of a column in? The story rated a top (that is top of a column). Time was certainly getting on. We had only a few more minutes, and the thought of remaking the page in that time seemed impossible. I walked back to the stone in a daze where the two stonehands were relaxing as if we had all the time in the world. One of them noticed my fright, thumbed out his cigarette and put it behind his ear and said, *Don't worry son, we'll do it*. They did, even helping me to write the headlines.

This was the exciting world which attracted me as a kid, bringing me back upstairs from the gym and baths. In those days the Night Editor was, I think, a Mr Russell. He was a Scotsman, a tall man with cropped hair and metal-rimmed glasses. He used the conference room, room 6, as an office. He was another imperturbable man, who spent much of his time out on the stone, but mostly I saw him in the late afternoon in the conference room. It was one of the nicest rooms in the office. It also had a coal fire and was booklined, and the big mahogany table and leather stuffed chairs gave it a clubbish air. The senior editorial men would meet there to prepare that night's paper, the selection and display of news and the discussion of leading articles. Occasionally, very occasionally, I had to take a message in during the early conference and always tiptoed as if I was in a cathedral. The conference was certainly as solemn. Nobody worked in shirtsleeves those days. Everybody wore dark formal clothes except for one eccentric leader writer who generally sat by the fire wearing green carpet slippers. He would walk to the office in them from his flat somewhere behind Victoria Street. Afterwards they would withdraw to their own comfortable offices unhurrying as if they did not have to produce a newspaper in a few hours or write a long leader on some political matter or foreign affair.

The old building, quiet behind its double windows and with its flickering coal fires, encouraged this gentlemanly approach to newspaper publishing, but it had long been too small. For instance, it was built, in the last century, without a room for reporters. They were then expected to write in the front hall where during the day classified advertisements were received. I suppose that reporters were not considered gentlemen. Even after the war, when I was a reporter, two or three of my older colleagues were not on the staff. They worked on space rates, so much a column. The reporters' room was in what was known as the Spiers and Pond Building to the west of the main building. It was reached by way of a footbridge, but the floor levels were different and one had to go up and down short flights of twisting stairs. The reporters were on the same floor as the correspondents of foreign papers which took *The Times* news service. Their room was irregularly shaped and looked like a tailor's sweatshop. Instead of desks there were benches coming out from the wall built by the house carpenter. Property east of the main building had also been taken over. This included a shop, where staff photographs were sold, and beyond the Eaton Building. The Sports Department was above the shop with lesser specialist writers, and the Art Department, Accounts and small departments were in the Eaton Building.

Architecturally, P.H.S. and its extensions were a mess. For a messenger it was an obstacle course because of the different floor levels and the stairs connecting one level to the next. Moving eastwards—I occasionally thought that a compass was necessary—say from one of the foreign papers, I would zigzag along a corridor between office partitions, up one flight of stairs, across the bridge, down another flight, then an abrupt right turn into the stair well of the main building, down a few more stairs, along the hushed corridor past the Editor's office in the main building, up some more stairs to above the shop, then up some more, another sharp right, and finally into the Eaton Building. In the shop block the corridor twisted by little offices hardly big enough for a table and chair. The door of one could not be fully opened when the occupant was sitting at his table. The corridors were badly lighted, and it was a relief in more ways than one to reach the Eaton Building. I sometimes hummed Excelsior when I reached its broad, cream-painted corridors. At the end of one of them was the Publicity Department, first a large general office and beyond a smaller room for Mr Casson, the departmental manager. One day I was told to report to him. He looked me up and down rather distastefully, and told me that I had been transferred to his department as an office boy. I was to report for work the following Monday at ten.

# 7

TWENTY YEARS before the Top People campaign the Publicity Department was an oddity in P.H.S. The paper depended of course on advertising revenue, but the top people on *The Times* were loath to advertise themselves or the paper. The assumption was that *The Times* did not have to be advertised. It was an institution, an essential part of national life, and with an assured readership. The circulation was only about 180,000, but given a small annual increase this was seen to be sufficient to attract enough advertisements to maintain financial independence and yield Major Astor a small return on his capital. The 180,000 paying readers were assumed to be top people. The phrase was never used, but the assumption was more confidently held than when it was coined after the war. However, it was recognized that advertising agencies had to be persuaded that they were arbiters of public taste and therefore cost more per column inch. The reduced subscriptions rate to undergraduates—as with the Jesuits *The Times* tried to catch them young—had to be made known. The columns of classified advertisements, the main source of revenue, had also to be maintained. Publicity was necessary, if not desirable.

The department also did not fit neatly into the P.H.S. hierarchy. Presumably Mr Casson was responsible to the Manager, but his staff were writers and artists and not accountants or clerks. The copywriters had come down from Oxbridge. The artists were vaguely bohemian. But if they could not be treated as clerks they certainly could not be regarded as editorial men. The consequence was a certain unease within the department. I discovered that most people resent not being one thing or another, certainly in an organization such as P.H.S., but long afterwards I realized that the department's indeterminate status helped me to make the first move into the editorial. If we were neither one thing nor another, we were halfway in between. The smallness of the department, and its tight budget, also helped. Mr Casson was happy enough to let me write advertizing copy as a 35-shilling-a-week office boy, and I also proved that I was not an illiterate.

Publicity was a pleasant department to work in, and one of the reasons I recognized later in Washington. There the status of the White House staff was measured by the distance of their offices from the oval room of the president. They fought for cramped attic rooms in the west and east wings rather than accept the large and lofty rooms in the Executive Building next door. At P.H.S., editorial men used the cramped little offices on the stairways while we had big rooms with plenty of light at the far end of the Eaton Building. At first I shared an office with Mr Binne, Mr Holt and Miss Tett. They each had a desk in a corner of the room, the door was at the fourth, and I sat at a long table in the middle. Copywriters such as Mr Holt and secretaries such as Miss Tett came and went. The secretaries got married. The copywriters were young, and did not intend to stay in the Publicity Department. For them it was a job rather like school-mastering, something to do after coming down from university while looking about for something better.

Mr Binne was different, which explained his assumed status as deputy to Mr Casson. He was an old soldier, and looked it with his straight back, trim moustache and carefully-brushed hair. I think he had come up through the printing trade, and perhaps he had nowhere else to go. He was to soldier on to retirement. Mr Binne must have been indispensible. Much of the department's work was the production of booklets and pamphlets requiring a good knowledge of type founts, printing processes, blocks, paper, layout and costing, and only he knew about them. Some of the booklets were expensively produced on heavy art paper, and showed how good he was with type. He was responsible for the double-crown bills put out each week for *The Times Literary Supplement*. He was also editor of the *House Journal* which he took very seriously. Mr Binne was kind to me. He would talk of his war years when he was in the horse artillery. He had a natural discipline, strengthened by his army service I suppose, and saw the world as a well-ordered society in which everybody had a place. He did not seem to resent the obvious fact that he would not succeed Mr Casson. He was content to live with his family in an Essex suburb and do his job as well as he could. He was fiercely loyal to the paper, but frequently inferred that it was not what it should be. This became a constant theme throughout my many years with *The Times*. Every critic was convinced that he knew what the paper had been in some long-lost golden age, and what it should become. Critics in recent years, mainly specialists trapped in their speciality, revealed as a God-given truth how the Editor or his deputies were ruining the paper. Mr Binne's complaint was that the paper somehow was not quite fulfilling its institutional role in that well-ordered society of his.

Mr Holt was different. He was the first middle-class Oxbridge man I got to know, or rather sat in a room with and listened to his conversation. He was very gentle, and with a shy smile behind his glasses. He did not take the work seriously, presumably because he did not have to, and eventually left to work for the War Graves Commission. His replacement was Mr Lucey, who came from Benson's, the advertising agents who did the Guinness ads. As he told it, Bensons attracted aspiring writers. Dorothy Sayers worked there. He had an ambition to write, but was killed in France soon after D Day. Miss Tett was one of those indeterminate ladies who could have been a clergyman's wife. She knitted. She eventually married, and was replaced by Miss Farquharson who looked and acted like the daughter of a sporting earl. She certainly had the assurance, accent and dash. She was a tall girl with dank blonde hair and long legs which I admired. She wore well-cut clothes and occasionally a monocle. She chain-smoked through a long holder, swore and made very funny jokes. She was not a good secretary, and did not care. She treated me as an equal, described the parties which left her with a hangover and urged me to become a reporter. The artists were in another room. Mr Barr, who was in charge, was a big Scotsman who smoked *Passing Cloud* cigarettes and drove a fast open touring car.

Again the work I was supposed to do was undemanding. I was expected to run messages in and out of the office and generally help the secretary, who was under-employed. At first I missed the company of other messengers, and the games and scuffles between our rounds, but it was a friendly office and I was accepted as one of them. Nobody objected when between my little chores I read the many magazines that came into the office. This was my first introduction to the *New Statesman*, the *Spectator*, the *Economist* and, above all, the *New Yorker*. I was captivated at the first read and have remained an addict ever since. I would keep it until Mr Casson came in grumbling about late deliveries. Eventually he became suspicious, and for a time I took it into his office after only glancing at the jokes and reading the Talk of the Town section. I also began to read *The Times* regularly for the first time. We had the old *News Chronicle* at home, which I secretly thought was the better paper. I especially enjoyed the Saturday weekend inset which was printed on green paper. I like the Robert Lynd essay and Vernon Bartlett, whom I accepted as an expert on international affairs. I told myself that the Diplomatic Correspondent of *The Times* was the better informed. I loyally reminded myself that *The Times* was the best paper in the world, but I found it hard going. And of course I objected to its policy towards Germany.

In the East End we were already concerned about Hitler. I suppose the large Jewish minority may have explained this, but it was not only a reaction to his persecution of the Jews. It was largely ideological, an obvious conflict between the Left and the Right. Fascist was a dirty word in Shadwell long before *The Times* stopped referring to the German dictator as Herr Hitler. But this did not diminish my respect for the paper. I suppose its history impressed me most: Russell at the Crimea was for me the essential *Times*. In my first weeks in the department I must have spent three or four hours a day reading the paper and these magazines. It was another education, I suppose. Certainly my horizon was broadened. After the *New Yorker*, I preferred the *New Statesman*. I developed a considerable respect and affection for Kingsley Martin, which I was happy to communicate to him when we first met in Lahore in 1947 where I was covering the mass migrations between India and Pakistan. We met again about two weeks later in New Delhi when I was invited to dine by the Governor General, Lord Mountbatten, at Government House. Kingsley, with his wife Dorothy Woodman, were house guests. It was a disastrous evening, and we often giggled about it when we met in later years.

Mountbatten had been the last Viceroy before becoming the first Governor General, a member of the Royal Family who obviously enjoyed living like a king. Government House provided a palatial background, almost certainly superior to Buckingham Palace, and the reception room where we met before dinner was swarming with ADCs in fancy regimentals. I had returned from the Punjab that morning overpowered by my experiences. For three or four weeks I had been based on Lahore, but moving about the divided province reporting the caravans of refugees and the massacres. One day I was driving through Amritsar, and had to stop on a bridge over the railway because of a mob swarming in the other direction. I waited, but every Sikh in the city seemed to be pouring over the bridge and the heat in the car became insupportable. I cautiously opened the door, and as I got out bumped into a Sikh with a *kirpan*, a short sword. The bloodlust was in him. His eyes were burning, and I thought he would decapitate me. Instead, he said, *I beg your pardon*, and ran on to help kill about 4,000 Muslim refugees in a siding below.

I stood on the bridge and watched until I was physically sick, and then drove back into the city to file the story. I went straight to the main post office, which was empty, and typed about a thousand words at the counter. They came out like hot lava. I found a couple of terrified Anglo-Indian telegraph clerks in the transmission room, and persuaded them to send the message to London. A few days later I returned to Delhi, mainly because of the invitation to Government House, but broke the journey at Umbala because I was tired. I also wanted a drink badly, and therefore went to the military cantonment instead of a Brahmin hotel in the city. I followed the signs to the officers' lines, stopped outside the bungalow of the commanding officer of the

1/11th Sikhs, and shouted *Koi hai*. A voice shouted to me to come in. It belonged to the C.O. who had just got out of the shower. We met in the hall, he with a towel round his middle and his hair tied in a top knot. I was told to fix a drink while he dressed. He returned in a freshly-laundered tennis shirt and slacks, and I explained myself. We had another drink, then he produced an airmail edition of *The Times* from the next room, and asked me if I had written the story about the massacre. We were anonymous in those days, and I could have said no. But I admitted authorship expecting to be shown the door. I could see the dinner, bath and bed disappearing. He looked at me pensively, and said that the other side was also guilty of bloodshed. I said that I knew, and had written about them. He nodded, and we went into dinner and talked about the old days.

His decent behaviour was very much on my mind when I was received by one of the ADCs at Government House, perhaps because the splendour of the room was in such theatrical contrast to the plain army-issued furniture of the colonel's bungalow and the dust and horror of the Punjab. I was introduced to other guests, given a drink and carefully placed to await the arrival of the Governor General and Lady Mountbatten. They were supposed to be living austerely because of the misery outside, but you would not have known it. He was dressed in uniform, she wore some kind of tiara, and the ADCs and servants outnumbered the guests. We waited where we had been placed until called to the presence or presences. Eventually my turn came to be led to Lady Mountbatten, and the ADC mentioned that I had just returned from the Punjab. She asked, *How are they treating my poor Hindus*? I was so astonished that I blurted out the last I had seen of them they were massacring 4,000 Muslim men, women and children. I was banished from the presence immediately, and led by the disapproving ADC to the nether part of the room and left with the teetotal Indian minister of some obscure department. Time dragged on. Kingsley had arrived, but not his wife. Mountbatten looked impatient and the ADCs alarmed. One of them discreetly scurried from the room. Finally, it seemed like hours, the enormous door opened a little, and Dorothy Woodman put her head round it. In a tiny voice she asked if she was late, and apologized. She had been listening to the birds coming in from the Jumna to settle in the trees, and had forgotten. The dissembling ADCs were a wonder to observe. So much for poor Lady Mountbanerjee, as she was then sometimes known. Earlier, when I read him in the Publicity Department, Kinglsey's preoccupation with India was a bit of a bore, but I enjoyed his Diary.

This reading-room life gradually diminished as I was drawn into the work of the department. It started with helping Mr Binne with the *House Journal*, and then because of my growing interest in typography he gave me some simple layouts to do. These were mostly for small four-page pamphlets designed to promote classified advertising, but I enjoyed doing them and was next allowed to help with the design of posters for *The Times Literary Supplement*. This was fascinating. In those days *The Times* had a Private Printing Office where much of this material was set and printed between large jobbing orders for outside customers, including H.M. Stationery Office. The PPO had a superb stock of type, rules and ornaments, and many of the comps were first-class craftsmen. They enjoyed producing fine work, and I spent a good deal of time down there ostensibly carrying out Mr Binne's corrections but also listening and agreeing to their suggestions. I would also take the final proofs to Mr Stanley Morison, who was then editor of the TLS. He was also working on the history of the paper, but retained his overlordship as typographer extraordinary.

He was a bit putting off at first. I had read about rusty black but had never seen it until I met him. He looked jesuitical, but had a nice smile behind his small, thick glasses and was kind to me. He had a way of completely disagreeing with the entire concept of a poster, and then reducing his criticism to what first appeared to be small points but which often radically changed and always improved the layout. He had a great feeling for space and a preference for simple rules. I can remember a comp in the PPO who shared my enthusiasm and found some rather complicated borders in a dusty unused case. They worked quite well the first time, on a TLS poster for the review of some French book. It was in two colours with a good block of a boulevard scene. Morison complimented me. It was a good poster, and I still have a copy of it. But he reacted strongly the next time I used a similar treatment, and of course he was right. The borders were fussy, and after some very firm words he advised me to use St Bride's library which then had a good collection of fount books. I became a regular visitor, and was well received as Mr Morison's young man.

The first newspaper ad which I did appeared in the old Paris edition of the *New York Herald Tribune*. The ad strongly reflected my historical approach to the paper. Headed *First in the Field*, it boasted that the paper was the first to establish an independent foreign news service, and so on. The copy was nothing special, but the combination of Bodoni Bold and Gill Sans with multiple straight rules still looks good. Mr Holt and then Mr Lucey were supposed to write the advertising copy, but they were often overworked when the decision was made to publish a house ad on Page 3 five days a week. The first three pages of the paper were then solid with classified advertising, and the little five-inch, single-column ad was intended to arouse reader interest in the paper's largest single source of revenue. They were supposed to be highly readable, and at one time the department persuaded itself that the Page 3 ad was comparable to the fourth leader and had a devoted readership. But it was a constant chore, and my first offering was willingly accepted. It appeared in *The Times* of June 22, 1936, under the heading *Admirable Crichtons*, as follows:

'If Lord Loam could possibly dispense with the services of his most admirable Crichton, that paragon would undoubtedly advertise for another post through *The Times* Classified Advertisements.

'The chances are unfortunately remote and meanwhile employers must content themselves with the servants of fact and not of fiction. Good servants are still to be found, however, although their numbers are regrettably few. What is more, they are sometimes in need of employment, for (as we know only too well) those less eligible may hold the posts which they deserve to occupy.

'They use *The Times* Classified Advertisements because it is the correct thing (and the wise thing) to do. Employers should read these columns for the same reason.

'Read *The Times* Classified Advertisements Every Day.'

I suppose that Mr Casson's reaction, when I took the copy into his office, was to have been anticipated. He had complete contempt for me and anybody who did not belong to his comfortable middle class, and showed it. His face was expressive under a shock of thick black hair, and dominated by thick hornrimmed glasses and a mobile mouth full of sharp teeth. He had a fashionable lisp. His sneer was so expressive that he ought to have been a film actor. I have forgotten what he said, but he read the copy slowly sneering the while. Then after a couple of changes, which of course I thought unnecessary, he threw the copy back at me, and snarled something about my being a budding writer. But as much as he disliked me, it soon became clear that my efforts were welcomed. After all, who else had a copywriter earning 35 shillings a week and still liable for office-boy duties? I followed this up quickly with a piece headed *Way of Escape*. It read:

' "Far from the madding crowd," however hackneyed and despised a phrase it may be, aptly describes the dreams of many business-tired men. In 1795 readers weary of town life found rest in the "neat and genteel dwelling house . . . situated in the agreeable and improving neighbourhood, South Lambeth" and in like properties that were advertised in *The Times* of that date. Nowadays, however, one must go farther than Lambeth to escape the "ignoble strife"—so far, indeed, that it seems the quest will never end. And yet the right place may be advertised in this very page of *The Times*— or perhaps it was snapped up a week ago, or perhaps it will be in the paper next week. You can never tell unless you keep a sharp look-out for these opportunities that occur often in *The Times* Classified Columns.

Read

*The Times*

Classified Advertisements

Every Day.'

I suppose I must have written more than 50 of these ads. They all assumed a life style which even then was passing, but the fact that I went home every night to the City of Dublin Dining Rooms in Shadwell never struck me as funny ha-ha, or funny odd. I was then a very serious political animal, toying with the idea of joining the Communist party, but I continued to write these pieces aimed at a group of people who enjoyed, or had enjoyed, what was considered to be the good life largely because of a system which exploited people such as myself. Many of the ads reflected the books I was reading at the time. For instance, on March 23, 1937, the Page 3 advertisment read:

'Sherlock Holmes, during one of his investigations, deduced that the ash he found in a man's pipe was proof that the owner of the pipe had lived in comfortable financial circumstances. From his wide knowledge of tobacco-ash (had he not written a monograph on the subject?) Holmes was able to identify the brand of the tobacco which, he explained patiently to Watson, had cost no less than eightpence an ounce!

'Besides this invaluable knowledge of peculiar and unknown subjects Holmes employed many other methods for nipping promising criminal careers in the bud. There were his amazing powers of observation; his band of street urchins called the Baker Street Irregulars; his pipe and coffee pot and finally the classified columns of a certain morning newspaper.

'In this "most amazing hunting ground for the student of the unusual" he discovered many clues that led to the solving of difficult problems.

'We ordinary mortals can also find an answer to our equally urgent questions if we

Read

*The Times*

Classified Advertisements

Every Day'

This work was done inside the department unknown to anybody outside. As far as the company was concerned I was still an office boy. But it improved my relations with Mr Binne, Mr Holt, Mr Lucey, and Miss Farquharson. It was about that time that she said I should become a reporter, but in a way the gap between me and the Editorial had become wider. As a front door messenger I had played at least a peripheral role in producing the paper. As an office boy-cum-unpaid copywriter I had joined the faceless, white-collar proletariat. I might as well have been on the moon, except my nebulous role did have its perks and did get me out of the office. Sir Harry Preston, then the manager of the Royal Albion Hotel in Brighton, wanted to advertise in the paper but did not have an advertising agent. I assume that a cut-rate deal was arranged, part of which was that *The Times* would write the ads. I prepared the first three of a series, six-inch, double-column advertisements, and took them down to Brighton for approval. I was supposed to return to my role as an office boy but Sir Harry, a splendid Edwardian character with a bald head and a large cigar, received me with a bottle of champagne, gave me a wonderful lunch, and said that the ads were fine. The first appeared on 5 November, 1936. Then I did a two-page spread in *The Times Review of Trade and Engineering*, long since defunct, for Hyderabad, or as the heading said, *The Dominions of His Exalted Highness the Nizam*. It was horrible, the worst kind of typography and commercial sycophancy, but by my eighteenth birthday I was almost fully employed as a copywriter. The pay was still that of a junior clerk, £2. 10s. od.

I was not impatient. Looking back now, I am amazed at my patience and genteel exploitation, but I was eager to write, and the Publicity Department was my best opportunity. I did pieces for the *House Journal*, but also looked outside for freelance work. This was available, as long as I kept my sights low and knew what to look for. A street accident or a fire always earned a few bob if immediately phoned in to one of the evening papers or morning populars. One night I went for a run along the Embankment with the Boxing Club and saw a fire on the scaffolding of Waterloo Bridge, which was being rebuilt at the time. As soon as I got back to the office I phoned in a few lines to the *Daily Express*, for which I was paid five shillings. I did not think of informing the Home News Department. Living in the East End was also a help. It was a mine of small paragraphs, which were often blown up afterwards into big stories. The coming and going of ships were regularly reported by local stringers, but tara. tula spiders among the bananas and other non-stories were always available. Then I would earn a few bob working on the edge of big stories such as the Charlie Brown murder. The reporters who came down from Fleet Street were nearly always willing to pay for leg work. They were very different from the men who worked for *The Times*. They seemed to wear a uniform, camelhair coats and snappy green hats, and I admired them enormously.

Other big stories were the Mosley-led fascist marches. The first was through the East End, and proved once again that a local man can often do better than a highly-paid special from outside. The East End was only a couple of miles from Fleet Street but was *terra incognita* for most of its provincially-born reporters. The Communist party, the Independent Labour Party and other groups were determined to stop the march. Tens of thousands of East Enders were persuaded to make a stand at Gardiner's Corner, a junction just east of Aldgate where the Commerical and Whitechapel roads divided. It was an impressive demonstration of working-class solidarity, and also quite bloody. In those days the police were firm when dealing with anybody not obviously belonging to the professional or middle classes. Not necessarily rough, not like a French flic or a New York cop, but they dealt firmly with the lower orders. They could be even harsher with left-wing demonstrators. Whatever Mosley stood for, and no matter the rabble at his heels, he was an obvious gentleman and patriot, which was more than you could say of the mob at Gardiner's Corner. We were Cockneys, unemployed, Jews, a few Irish, and I suppose some agitators. We shouted, *They shall not pass*, and were no doubt seen as dangerous revolutionaries. We were also blocking the King's Highway to legitimate traffic, which included Mosley's bully boys who had police permission to march through the East End although their intention was clearly provocative. It must have infuriated Sir Philip Game, the then Metropolitan Police Commissioner, who appeared in uniform mounted on a horse. When the mob refused to disperse, he ordered the mounted police to charge. They did, and with unusual brutality. If any reader thinks this is an exaggeration, I still have a scar on my forehead to prove it.

The large roundabouts which have reduced the area to an automotive desert did not exist in those days, and the police trotted down from the Underground station swinging their loaded batons indiscriminately. A line of resisters disappeared with each charge, and those in rear surged back. The crush became intolerable, and eventually I was swept back against one of the plate-glass windows of Gardiner's store. Next to me an old Jew kept saying, *Don't push, don't push*, but the mob was out of control. Suddenly the glass cracked and we all fell in. It was like the lifting of a safety valve. The mob loosened and the police broke through. Miraculously I had not been cut by glass, but a baton struck my forehead and for a while I could hardly see for blood. I was struck a second time on the shoulder, and I was conscious of the copper wheeling his horse to come at me again when he was distracted by the looting of Mr Gardiner's scotch woollens. I was then rounded up with dozens of others and taken to Leman Street police station. Fortunately I had phoned in a couple of stories before the cossacks charged, and one got a big play in the old *Star*. Some cab drivers, most of them Jews, had organized themselves as a mobile column to ferry reinforcements from one street to another and to retrieve the wounded. I compared them with the Paris cab drivers who rushed French troops to the Marne in 1914. The rewritten story ran for about two-thirds of a column.

The Mosley march through south-east London was more profitable. This time the resisters adopted more effective tactics. Instead of presenting a solid but vulnerable front as in the East End, numerous commando forces made sallies from side streets and alleys. The many railway bridges across the streets were ideal for ambuscades. The resisters waited behind the low brick walls until the head of the procession had passed underneath and then pelted the remainder with stones from the permanent way. The police were helpless. I knew south-east London fairly well because of my earlier walks to the swimming pool in Southwark park. I phoned in four or five stories and eventually collected the equivalent of a week's pay.

By this time I was grateful for the leisurely pace of the Publicity Department. Apart from freelancing at the most vigorous and lowest-paid level, I was still boxing, taking girls out, going to the theatre and attending night school. At first I went to the night school off Kingsway which *The Times* expected me to attend. The course was designed for the white-collar proletariat, simple double-entry bookkeeping, shorthand and typing. The last two subjects were useful, but it was too much like a conditioning or programming for *Untermenschen*. I transferred to Goldsmiths' College where I took French and a course known as the Art of Writing. It was in New Cross, south of the river and at the end of the

District Line. It is now part of London University, but was then a good example of the old LCC Night Classes. An extraordinarily wide range of subjects was available. Given sufficient application and the Underground railway any ambitious or earnest lad could get a good education and learn carpentry or metalwork on the side.

Goldsmiths' was a handsome red brick building which deserved a better setting than the trams which then used to grind by. The catchment area, to use the modern jargon, covered most of south London judging from the distances and directions I travelled taking girls home. At various times I went from Eltham in one direction to Crystal Palace in another. The journeys always ended outside a semi-detached house. I was never invited in. Lower-middle-class convention prevented that until you were going steady, but it revealed a new world which I had only glimpsed at Isleworth. My previous wanderings through London had never taken me through inner suburbia. I had known Belgravia better than Lewisham. It was fashionable to sneer at suburbia, even in Shadwell, but it looked fine to me. I was particularly impressed by the neat little front gardens, the hedges and the young trees planted in the streets, or rather in the roads, avenues and crescents. Even the names did not seem ridiculous. The Acacia Roads were so obviously different from High Street, Shadwell, that they deserved posh names. I saw them generally only after nightfall, which may have improved them. The lighted, curtained windows looked cosy, even if upper-floor windows were cluttered with the obligatory three-mirror dressing table. In the spring, at the end of the school year, the roads were bright with flowers and the paintwork, mostly green and cream, looked trim.

The girls were an eye-opener too. Perhaps they were not so pretty as East End girls, whose Cockney, Irish and Jewish faces also provided infinite variety, but they were then just beyond a little class barrier. Most of them spoke with what I suppose was a Home Counties accent. The aspirates slipped occasionally, but their voices were what our mother called refined. Their clothes were plainer, a tendency to woollen jumpers and twin sets rather than the coloured *crêpe de Chine* blouses of Shadwell on a Saturday night. There was also the suggestion of a life unknown in the East End, of tennis clubs more social than sporting, of standards and expectations parallel, if a long way apart, to middle-class life as presented in books and gossip columns. The parallelism may have been illusory, but it assumed a security unknown to most East Enders. In economic terms it was the difference between a small but regular income of about £5 or £6 a week and the two or three quid, irregular and without guarantee, of the casual docker. The financial difference was not so narrow as it would now seem, but it was the assumption of a regular income that mattered most. Given this, they could buy a semi for about £700 on a mortgage. They could acquire furnishings and decent clothes. They might be strapped until the children were old enough to work. Their lives might be comparatively colourless and emotionless, as assumed by middle-class writers, but they lived in a different world from the East End. They lived in its nether regions but could identify with those above.

This probably explained the French classes. They had all taken French at their secondary schools and were determined to improve it, largely in the expectation of spending a holiday on the continent. It was always the continent, and not France, and the definite article made it sound superior and mysterious, as it did to the Argentine and the Sudan in later years. I don't know if they ever went. This was years before packaged tours, and Clovelly was the limit of most lower-middle-class ambition, but it was apparently necessary to assume that one day they would spend a couple of weeks in Nice or Cannes. Holidays were, however, only one reason for learning French. France, and all things French, loomed largely in their imagination. Anything French, or almost anything, was assumed to be the best, and of course the French were supposed to be more sophisticated than the English. Again this was parallelism at work. In those days France was culturally dominant. Those girls merely reflected middle and upper-middle class assumptions, and in so doing raised a little more that class barrier between us. For in Shadwell we yielded to nobody, and certainly not the French. France meant the first world war and the mythology of gallant British soldiers being charged for drinking water. The French were Frogs. In any event, too many were connected with the sea to be excited by foreign parts. Nevertheless, most of them were nice girls, ultimately different from those I knew in Shadwell in that they could have, or thought they could have, aspirations for better things. Most of them also were warm human beings, longing for the warmth of others. By today's standards they were certainly inhibited, and their warmth was not indiscriminate. My children would no doubt snigger if they knew the details, but my brief and inconclusive affairs in trams and buses careering over south London, or in some shadow near the ancestral semi were occasionally wonderfully and mutually warm.

Perhaps because of this extracurricular activity I can't remember too much about Goldsmiths'. I had learned only German at St George's and found French hard going. Perhaps the sperm of my German grandfather was stronger than that of the French Basque. In any event, because of the large number of young girls the atmosphere of the French class was never really serious. Dating rather than linguistic ability came first. The art of Writing class was very different. Many more students were earnest. They wanted to learn, but their earnestness was not rewarded. How do you teach people to write? I can't recall the instructor asking that question. The assumption was that writing could be taught as easily as carpentry, and the error created considerable tension. The analysis of contemporary writing produced only sneers. It eventually dawned on me that many of my fellow students were frustrated writers. They were convinced that only they could write. Published writers pandered to popular taste or were publishers' in-laws.

Much of the talk about new movements went above my head. I assumed that writing was a matter of communicating, and that stories should have a beginning, middle and end. Somerset Maugham was then one of my heroes, and I was to discover afterwards how well he had communicated the lives of British expatriates in Malaysia and south-east Asia generally. Most of them were also based on true stories though the locations had been changed, presumably to avoid libel actions. For instance, a Singapore incident was retold with Penang or Alor Star as the background. When I was *The Times* south-east Asia correspondent one of my hobbies was to track down the origins of these stories, and I was fairly successful because some of the people involved, or who had known about them, were still alive. Memory did not make Maugham popular. On one occasion I was in Chiang Mai in Thailand for a few days. The Chinese hotel was unliveable because of the constant music and the British consul suggested that I ought to stay at the club. It was a pleasant place down by the river, and he took me down one day to meet the secretary. He was a charming old man, who had worked too many decades in the teak forests to contemplate home retirement. Drinks were ordered, we chattered of this and that, and especially about tennis. There was no suggestion that I would not be welcomed, until the consul mentioned that I was a correspondent of *The Times*. The response could not have been more dramatic if the consul had dropped his trousers or insulted the monarch. The *bonhomie* disappeared as he ejaculated, *No, not another scribbling chap like that bounder Maugham.* It took a great deal of explaining before I was reluctantly admitted, and then only on my solemn oath that I would write nothing about the club or its members. He was very friendly afterwards, and a great help when I moved west into the hills of Burma to report on American military support for the Nationalist Chinese troops there, but that is another story.

At Goldsmiths' the writers were scornful of Maugham and of my uneducated ideas about writing. A piece I had done for *The Times House Journal* was analysed and found wanting, but it must have been better received elsewhere because the Home Editor in P.H.S. asked me to do a story for the paper. King Edward had abdicated, and P.H.S. was preparing to cover the coronation of King George the Sixth. *The Times* always covered such occasions supremely well, perhaps because it took them seriously. At that time men such as Dermot Morrah were on the staff, and with their deep knowledge and awareness of history as well as royal ceremonial they were well equipped to write the great set pieces. But full treatment was to be given to all the day's festivities, and apparently before the News Editor got to the end of the list every man had been deployed. I was asked to cover the street parties in the East End. They could not have chosen a better man, even if I say so myself. On the East End I was no less an expert than was Dermot Morrah on the House of Windsor. I was told to keep it down to half a column, about 500 words.

It was my first assignment for *The Times*, but except for a warning to have my copy in by 7 p.m. this auspicious beginning for the paper and myself went unnoticed. Even in the Publicity Department where Mr Lucey had also been pressed into service. He attracted most of the attention and congratulations, perhaps because it was well established that he could write. Had he not reviewed the Mus. and Dram. productions for the *House Journal*? This perhaps sounds bitchy, but that is not my intention. He was too nice a person, and almost certainly would have become a good writer if he had not been killed in France. The point I'm trying to make is that as an office boy I slipped through the departmental divisions unnoticed. I was permitted to write advertising copy because the department was understaffed. I was allowed to write my first story for the paper for much the same reason. Rather than being bitchy, I am in retrospect very grateful. Today it would be almost impossible to make such a sureptitious upward journey from the bottom. The Editorial Department is still not a closed shop but the National Union of Journalists effectively influences recruitment. A reporter cannot be hired unless he has served his apprenticeship elsewhere. Between the wars recruitment was very haphazard. Reporters generally came from the provincial press, as they do today, but bright young graduates were recruited directly from Oxbridge for the foreign side. They would spend a year or so in Letters or with the *Educational Supplement*, and then be sent abroad. The system had its drawbacks, but worked better than it should have done. The new system has increased professionalism, but it is a pity that recruitment from the bottom is now impossible. No doubt poor but bright boys have better opportunities in the welfare state. They can go to university and enter journalism through the front door, but the American experience shows that Harvard Ph.Ds do not necessarily make good reporters. Journalism, like acting and prostitution, is not a profession but a vocation. You either have what it takes, or you don't, and general experience shows that some of the best journalists, those who can write and instinctively know what is news, began as copy boys or printers' devils.

Professionalism and the unions are not entirely to blame, at least on *The Times*. The old paternalism and loyalty have disappeared. They went long before Lord Thomson took over the paper. The postwar changes in British life no doubt explain much, but the turning point in the history of the paper was when it was struck in the mid-fifties. For the first time since 1785 the paper did not come out. Even during the General Strike a small paper was got out, but in the fifties the presses were silent for a month. They were silenced not by the old craft unions, but by the electricians who did not share the special loyalty of printers to the paper. For them P.H.S. was just another plant which needed electricians to maintain equipment. If the paper failed they could always get another job, in another kind of plant. It was the first of many industrial disputes which eventually demolished the concept of the Companionship. No doubt the attitudes of the proprietors were also changing. The Astor family had been exposed to postwar change, especially in the tax laws. Lord Astor was required to move abroad to save the family fortune in America from death duties. Inevitably the son did not inherit his fathers' ideas, although he was a friendly man and a good employer. The Hever Days did not survive the war, and many other staff activities disappeared or were reduced. The new building may have had less obvious effects upon the staff. Acres of glass and open plan might have let in more light and rationalized work, but human relationships seem to flourish better in fire-lit rooms and dark passages. Whatever the reasons, a messenger today can't hope for the kind of advancement possible during the more class-conscious years between the wars. It is now a dead-end job and the boys behave accordingly.

This is not to infer that before the war every messenger carried an editorial pen in his delivery tray. Few thought of making the jump, and fewer succeeded. It was also a lengthy process. My first story for the paper remained the only story for a long time, which may explain why I remember it so clearly and why the preparations were so thorough. I read the local paper for coronation news and spent a couple of evenings on reconnaissance. When the great day dawned I equipped myself with a new notebook, the badge of the ardent and self-conscious beginner. Later I rarely used a notebook and often forgot to carry a pen. The pretence was that they spoilt the hang of my jacket. Then it developed into a silly but inoffensive vanity. For instance, in Washington at one of my regular meetings with Dean Rusk, then the Secretary of State, we were sipping Scotch as usual (for some reason the steward always served him with three to my two) when he said something which I had to get down correctly. I asked to borrow his pen and scribbled a note on the cocktail napkin. He was amused, and it was one of those inconsequential incidents which always enhance one's reputation when told by a cabinet officer. But that was many years later.

In 1937 I went off to Shadwell fully equipped and inspected the street parties as if I was a visitor from a distant planet. I looked at two or three and then decided to do a set piece and chose Juniper Street. It was the best choice for many reasons although one could not be mentioned that day. Or so I decided. (My first act of self-censorship?) Juniper Street was a small turning off Glamis Road, narrow and lined on both sides by tall tenement houses. It had a fair claim to being the most densely populated street in London. During daylight the street literally swarmed with people, most of them children. I cannot remember seeing so many in one place until I went to Calcutta. Presumably this explained why it was always known as Incubator Street. A gross slander of its worthy people no doubt, but so many fecund families were packed into the tenements that they did look like incubators. Juniper Street was also part of the Glamis estate which was owned by the Bowes-Lyon family. The woman who was crowned queen that day was a Bowes-Lyon. The contrast was absolute. The wealth and well-being of that smiling woman— who I am sure was a decent, good-hearted woman—depended in part on rents from some of the worst slum property in London.

That day the slumdwellers were not resentful, if they ever were. Their patriotism was unquestioned, and in any case they were determined to enjoy themselves. The day was a public holiday and the children did not go to school. For the fathers it was a day of compulsory unemployment. The docks were also closed, which meant that they all went unpaid. Nevertheless, they were determined to enjoy themselves. Flags and paper decorations were strung across the street. Tables and chairs had been brought down from the tenements and set in a continuing, irregular line down the middle of the road. Groups of mothers got together to spread bread with margarine and jam or bloater paste, and pour tea. The pavements were lined with crates of brown ale. The local talent performed on a stage at one end, and everybody sang. It was a very good party, so good that it was gone six and approaching my deadline when I reluctantly decided that the time had come to write. It was too late to get back to the office, and I wrote my story sitting at a table with a bottle of brown ale at my elbow. I then went off to a public call box, phoned P.H.S.

and asked for the Home Telephonists. I have forgotten the name of the man in charge. He was a thin man with a limp, eternally bad-tempered because of an old wound. He was also very busy that night. When I got through and announced myself, he said, 'Christ, they're even using f—king office boys today. They'll have the cleaners next.'

IN THE summer of 1937 our mother announced that we were to move from Shadwell, not to the promised land of Bromley or Beckenham but about half way to Crofton Park. This was a shabby inner suburb indistinguishable from much of south-east London except by the surrounding cemeteries. The house we moved to was at the end of a terrace in Dalrymple Road, a 20-minute ride by Southern Electric to Blackfriars or half-an-hour on a 74 tram. It was a typical late-Victorian dwelling with three floors in front and two behind. The bay windows and exterior ornaments were fussy, but the house was roomy and with plenty of light. The downstairs backroom overlooking the strip of garden, which we used as a sitting and dining room, was a delight after the living room in Shadwell. With eight rooms and a bathroom, the house represented a definite improvement in living standards although our mother let the two top rooms to a young couple.

Leaving Shadwell was a wrench because it meant the breakup of our Hindu-style family. Uncle Lou and Mary stayed behind and eventually married, a happy event which should have taken place years before. Uncle Lou depended upon her, and she had given him affection of the no-nonsense kind as well as constant attention. They moved to a little council flat in Bewley Buildings, where they lived throughout the war, and afterwards in Chancery Buildings. Both blocks were within a hundred yards of the shop. They were very happy until Uncle Lou died in 1972. The move also precipitated the marriage of Beatie, who returned to Shadwell. Jim stayed behind. Old Tom came along because he had nowhere else to go. His future was not discussed. He just came, like an uncomprehending and dependent child.

Our numbers were reduced from eight to four, and soon to three when old Tom died. The change was drastic, but was welcomed on the whole. The house in Shadwell had become much too small. Until the move, Beatie was still sleeping with our mother, and I was sharing a bed with Bill. The one lavatory posed an obvious problem which chamber pots could not completely resolve. Bill had begun night work, and after eight in the morning sleep in Shadwell High Street was almost impossible because of the noise. Beatie was courting, and apart from the shop after hours she and her boyfriend had no place to be alone in. The upstairs front room was used only on Sundays until the end. We had in fact more room than most families in the neighbourhood. Most of my friends lived in tenements, which had one or two bedrooms, a living room and kitchen, or in by-law cottages not much bigger. They had two rooms up and two down with a scullery at the back. The downstairs back, with its coalburning oven, was kitchen, dining and living room. The only light was a gas jet protruding from the wall near the oven. The rooms were much smaller than ours. But overcrowding was not the only reason why we were glad to go. Our mother had her ambitions, and Bill and I had grown out of Shadwell much earlier.

The process had begun with our mother, who had always assumed that we would leave, and with the tenuous connexion with *The Times*. For her a good job in the print and a house in Bromley or Beckenham meant security, respectability and keeping yourself to yourself. St George's school, the BBC.

and the public library had also been part of the process. They created for me a secret world in which my imagination roamed, undisciplined perhaps but with very little baggage. I'm not sure that I would have entered that world so freely if I had been born in Beckenham or Bromley. Their schools and libraries were no doubt good, but living opposite the London Docks and listening to ships' sirens at night may well have been an indispensable beginning. Those sirens may have led me also to wandering and working abroad for a quarter of a century. Even now, when I am supposed to be middle-aged and settled, I hear them, and they still lead me to faraway places, to China and Brazil.

Perhaps the move to Crofton Park was the first essential step of what was to prove to be a long journey, but for all our eagerness to go Shadwell was not a bad place when we did leave. Conditions had improved, if only marginally. There was more work in the docks, and therefore more money to spend. Slum clearance had reduced the basic squalor a little. Families moving out of the neighbourhood as they made good also reduced the pressure on housing. We were certainly not the first to go among the people we knew. Some Jewish families had already left for Finchley or Golders Green. But perhaps the improvement was more personal than general. Certainly our mother was much better off with three children working. She must have been relatively well off with her earnings from the shop and our weekly contributions. Not that we saw too much in return. She must have been saving for the move, but she could afford to be a little less tight. Delicacies such as cockles and shrimps appeared more often at Sunday teatime. An evening glass of Guinness was no longer unusual, although she remained frugal and the bottle was hastily put away if somebody called. On their Saturday nights up west Uncle Lou and Mary went to the

Cumberland Hotel for supper instead of a Lyons Corner House.

If we were better off than most of our neighbours, the general improvement could not be entirely explained by more ships in the docks and slightly less overcrowding. As the Irish immigrants had settled down drunkenness became less frequent. When I was a boy the police were invariably called in to stop the Saturday night rowdiness at the *Lord Lovat* next door and the *Gunboat* along the street. Such brawling was rare by the time we left. The Jewish immigrants had done well as a group. Those who had not departed for Golders Green had improved their shops and tailoring establishments. Their sons still staggered aboard trams and buses heavily laden with completed garments for posh shops up west. These were the products of the sweatshops, but other sons had graduated to cars with racks in the back for suits and dresses. Still others had opened their own wholesale shops along the Commercial Road or smart retail shops such as Cecil Gee. With the Irish, they had also been assimilated. Some even frequented a pub, the *Eagle* I think, in the Commercial Road. Thus the underlying tensions had been relaxed. Earlier there had been no violence because of the ability of the poor to live with each other. Later, the Fascist marches revealed a solidarity all the more powerful because it was not the product of some race relations board.

The beginnings of the consumer society also helped. The old grocery shops with their few essentials sold from open bins and barrels were giving way to the chain stores. Sainsburys still sold butter from casks, patted into half-pounds by shop assistants armed with square-shaped wooden bats, but more packaged goods and a greater variety were made available. Sainsburys and Home & Colonial also imposed standards of hygiene unthought of previously. Of course the little corner shops away from the street markets still flourished, not only because of convenience but also because regular customers were allowed to buy food on tick. The old dairies survived with one or two cows kept in the yard behind. I can remember one near St George's church which would not have looked out of place in a village. In the summer months it sold glasses of milk and soda for a penny. It always looked cool and clean, and the brasses of the yellow milk cart and its pony were always polished. But the milk was served from door to door from a large urn into metal cans, and the quality must have been uncertain. The milk sold in sealed bottles by the commercial dairies was becoming increasingly popular, and certainly tasted better.

Readymade clothes were also becoming readily available. Marks & Spencers had yet to make a mark in Stepney, but we all knew about Burtons, 'The Tailors of Taste', and the Fifty Shilling Tailors. I went to Burtons for my annual suit, presumably because it cost only thirty-seven shillings and sixpence. I went to the branch in the Strand, near Charing Cross station, and it was always an event. It looked like a gentleman's tailoring establishment with its well made counters and cabinets. The assistants were polite, and the impression of personal service was carefully maintained. I suppose the suits were mass produced, but alterations were made and I could boast that my suits were tailormade. The cloth was heavy, because our mother always insisted upon hardwearing clothes, but the quality was good. At least my new suits, after being kept for Sunday best until I had grown out of the last one, stood up to constant wear. My brother, who was older and had more money, went to Cecil Gee where the prices were higher but the tailoring sharper.

This was also the heyday of the super cinemas, and the Roxy in the Commerical Road certainly led to an improvement in our life style. I had been a regular cinema goer since watching serials at a Methodist church-hall for a penny every Friday night. I graduated to the tuppenny fleapits and the free seats in the Paleseum. I can still remember my first talkies, a splendid double feature of *All Quiet on the Western Front* and *Broadway Melody*. This of course was before television—except for the fortunate few—and the cinema was more than an escape. It was adventure, excitement and romance comparable to Robert Louis Stevenson and Hemingway, but the Roxy raised the cinema to a great social occasion. Like Burtons, only more so, the Roxy treated us as if we were socialites and patrons of the arts and good living. Instead of hole-in-the-wall fleapits, dirty and unkempt, the Roxy truly was a pleasure dome. Its sheer size was impressive, and the comfortable seats, pile carpets, smart usherettes and overwhelming décor had an extraordinary effect upon most of us. We dressed up, put on our best suits and dresses, to go to the Roxy. We went with the highest expectations and were rarely disappointed. From the moment the mighty Wurlitzer arose from the depths, with the organist smiling in the revolving spotlights, until the end of the second feature was a continuing delight.

The old life continued, the going to church, the friendliness of the streets, the visits to relatives and the occasional treat up west. Beer was still brought from the pubs in jugs. The fish-and-chip shops were still the most constant supply of protein, although they then competed with the pie shops. Why pie shops have since almost disappeared while fish-and-chips have become a national and exportable institution is a mystery I cannot fathom. Whatever the meat content, and it always looked grayish, the rather salty and rubbery pie crust was superb. I would chew upon it for what seemed a heavenly eternity. The pies were sold with mashed potatoes, the whole covered in parsley sauce. They cost no more than fish-and-chips. Two and a pennyworth was the standing order—tuppence for the pie and a penny for the mashed. They had to be carried home in a bowl instead of newspaper, but were well worth the trouble. Other traditional delights were still readily available, and perhaps more plentiful because of the slow increase in living standards. Special favourites were the whelks-and-cockles stalls which stood in most street markets and at some prominent corners every Saturday night and Sunday morning. They were covered with clean white sheets or tablecloths, and the costermonger wore a blue-and-white striped apron and often a boater, or flat straw hat. The whelks and cockles were sold in little saucers. You helped yourself to vinegar, salt and pepper, and ate them with your fingers standing at the stall. If you were flush you could have jellied eels for tuppence a plate, spitting out the bones into the gutter. Live eels were also sold, which our mother used to cook with parsley and potatoes, and shrimps and cockles for Sunday tea. A few stalls sold oysters for two shillings a dozen.

I talked to an old lady in a pub off Cable Street one night soon after the war, and she remembered those few brief years before the war as the best days of her life. I don't think that she was overly sentimental. They were good days in spite of the continuing poverty, and I certainly enjoyed them. I was growing up fast. The job at *The Times* was proving to be interesting, and I assumed that I would get on. I was not quite sure what it meant, but I had no doubts as to the future. I was a chip off the old block in that I had inherited our mother's confidence. I had money to spend, and London was at my doorstep. I drifted from the sea scouts to the Old Vic, where a gallery seat cost 6d., and to Sadlers Wells which cost 9d., or 1s. 3d. in the amphitheatre when I wanted to impress a girl. The commercial theatres were a bit more expensive but not much if you lined up for the Gods, or gallery. Apart from economic necessity, I enjoyed the Gods because I believed the old myth that the actors played to us and not the stodgy occupants of more expensive seats below. My theatre-going was as indiscriminate as my reading. In the winter I went twice a week, to light comedy, Shakespeare, musicals, Restoration plays, Italian and eventually German opera, ballet and symphony concerts.

I went to music halls in the East End whenever a good turn appeared. Sophie Tucker was the favourite, but I can remember going to a hall down near Poplar when a circus appeared on the stage. It was good enough fun until an elephant appeared when it became hilarious. The elephant peed, seemingly unendingly, and it emptied into the orchestra where the musicians gallantly played on. I remembered their gallantry years later, in 1954 to be exact, when the Queen visited Ceylon during a world tour. I had come down from Delhi, where I was stationed, to help wherever possible Bob Cooper, the *Times* man covering the tour. He was a superb writer, and needed little help. But he was a slow writer, which created problems for him as a journalist and led both of us, if separately, into an awful predicament the night the Kings of Kandy and their elephants marched past the monarch. Being too late to reach the saluting stand we had to march, carrying our portable type-writers, behind the elephants. Fortunately I have a poor sense of smell, but my shoes and trousers were ruined.

I enjoyed the circus as much as Wagner, and both for less than today's price for a packet of cigarettes. I lined up at the gallery doors, often in dank cold, and occasionally walked home for want of tuppence for a bus fare. But I can't remember feeling poor or deprived. How could I with all this wonderful magic within easy reach?

I continued to sit in the gallery or amphitheatre when I made more money, but ate out before or after the show. The brasserie in the Lyons Corner House at Trafalgar Square was a favourite place. The building with its floors of restaurants and tearooms was very posh by my standards. With Burtons and the Roxy it catered for what are called the masses, gave us our moneysworth, lifted us out of snack bars and caffs and performed a social service which is still not generally recognized. The brasserie in the basement was informal with check tablecloths, Italian pepper pots and waiters in white aprons. A band played romantic music, often the better-known Italian arias, and the strings would stroll between the tables serenading pretty girls and tired old mums. Often I had to line up, as for the gallery, but once inside there was all this and a good meal for two or three shillings. The *hors d'oeuvres* trolley was enormous, and very good. A helping cost 1s. 6d. I got to know a Cockney waiter who would pile my plate and give me a foot or so of French bread. It may not have been a balanced diet, but I ate it with gusto once or twice a week.

When I was feeling flush, and had a very pretty girl, I would go to a restaurant in Charlotte Street, to Schmidt's, Bertorelli's or Antoine's. I preferred Schmidt's, perhaps because of our mother's German background I liked wurst, kraut and beer, and Schmidt's was cheap. But Antoine's was the place which impressed girls. It seemed very French. The set three-course meal cost 3s. 6d., and a half bottle of wine about 3s. With coffee and tip the total was about thirteen shillings. It was a great deal of money, but the food was good and the girls were always impressed. Occasionally, depending upon the girl, we would go to the Fitzroy Tavern. I now know that Dylan Thomas began to drink himself to death there, but then he was only one of the many nameless chaps who wrote, or thought they could write, and enthused for hours over a few pints of bitter at that scruffy bar.

I did not then know of him. I was unaware that he had written and had published *Eighteen Poems* and *Twentyfive Poems*. I knew very little of what was going on at the time. I was from the outside. I was still catching up and without knowing that I was coming up from behind. Nearly everything I saw, heard or read was a new experience, an exciting discovery. Beethoven, Mozart, Wagner, Bach, Tchaikovsky and Dvorak did not exist before I heard them, first on the BBC and at school and then on the concert and operatic stage. The effect could be overwhelming. I can still remember the sheer exaltation of hearing Beethoven played live for the first time; and of staggering away in a drunken state from Covent Garden with Wagner swelling from within me as I walked down the Aldwych and Fleet Street to St Paul's, then along Cannon Street to London Bridge and the Tower and eventually home. I had the price of a bus fare in my pocket, but could not have sat still with the excitement. Then there was the delight of watching *Les Sylphides* danced for the first time and the exotic flourish of *Aida* at Sadlers Wells.

To much of this I came unequipped and unprepared in spite of the efforts of Mr Reece at St George's and the BBC's *Foundations of Music*. I heard such music live because it was there, to be had for a few coppers and within a bus ride or walking distance from Shadwell. Similarly I was thrilled—there is no other word—by Olivier and Richardson and other great players at the Old Vic. I tried to tell Sir Ralph about it years later at a supper party after a first night in the United States. I don't think he understood. We had both come a long way—he very much farther—from the prewar unfashionable Old Vic. But Lilian Baylis would have understood.

I was one of the faceless Cockneys she was determined to improve, but I also lined up for Coward and middle-class plays such as *George and Margaret* and *Escape Me Never*.

Much of this would have been beyond me if I had not lived in a place such as Shadwell, but of course it took me out of Shadwell. The old well-defined boundaries of the parish had disappeared before we moved to Crofton Park. I had crossed them too often, to a job at *The Times* instead of in the docks, to the City of London sea scouts, and by way of the public library and those ships' sirens. Hence the relative painlessness of the move. It did not seem to matter where I lived as long as it was near the Underground or Southern Electric, and the house had a bathroom. Crofton Park left no impression, except for the memory of for the first time not having to share a bedroom. We moved the following year to Beckenham where our mother bought a small semi on a mortgage. She made it to the promised land, and only just in time. The war came in the following year, and first I and then my brother joined the army. The shop in Shadwell disappeared in the first blitz and the house in Crofton Park was also destroyed. It was just as well that our mother wanted to move to Bromley or Beckenham, although the semi was badly damaged by a flying bomb. We never lived as a family again. After the war my brother married and moved to Huntingdonshire, our mother retired to a bungalow in Birchington in Kent, and I joined an exclusive fraternity of international tramps by becoming a foreign correspondent. I spent almost a quarter of a century wandering about the world. My children were born in Singapore, Delhi, Bonn and Washington. A family joke has it that wherever we land we always have to join the aliens' queue at immigration.

I made the switch easily enough. The war helped of course. During nearly seven years in the army I served from the

Arctic Circle to the Equator, from Akureyri in Iceland to Kunming in China. I learned to use a knife and fork at Sandhurst and in various officers' messes. After the war it seemed only too easy to go on travelling, from the Indian subcontinent to the Middle East, to Southeast Asia, to Europe and the United States, and many places in between. I served as the fire brigade man covering instant crises, as resident correspondent in most continents, as war correspondent, as special correspondent, as the chief correspondent in Washington and eventually as American Editor before returning home at the end of 1970 to become deputy editor and foreign editor. It was a long way to come from the City of Dublin dining rooms, but I never shook off Shadwell or my Cockneyness.

In the early days it made some people uneasy, especially British ambassadors abroad. A foreign correspondent of *The Times* was not expected to speak Cockney. Of course the accent is atrocious, as bad if not worse than Geordie and the German spoken in Lower Saxony, but it was also a signal that I was not one of them. I did not respond in a conditioned or programmed way to situations and events. I could never understand why certain things were left best unsaid or not done. Moreover, eighteen years lived in the East End had hardly persuaded me that the Establishment knew what was best for me and the rest. I was a populist, which helps to explain why I felt at home in the United States, but I served fifteen years abroad before being posted to Washington. Fortunately I spent most of my time with foreigners who did not seem to mind about my speaking or trying to speak their language with a Cockney accent. The accent changed over the years. In the United States women even said, *Gee, I just love your British accent*. But a Dr Higgins would still recognize my background from the way I speak. I tend to turn simple declarative statements into tentative questions. For instance, I don't say *It's a nice day* but *It's a nice day, isn't it?* The odd Cockney expression still slips out.

Neither the accent nor the attitude mattered at *The Times*. Journalists tend to be classless, and I was readily accepted as a colleague by the superior Oxbridge men who then ran the paper. Donald Tyerman, who gave me my first chance after the war, is a Yorkshireman. Other senior men were from Scotland. Mine was just another regional accent. I was judged by my reporting, and I was a good reporter. I am a natural journalist, and my Cockney experience and attitude made me a better one. They often got me and the paper into trouble, but I was always loyally defended. Dr Adenauer called me a *Drahtzieher*, or wirepuller. Powerful representations were made to Cabinet Office when Templer was High Commissioner of Malaya. More than once I was accused of being a communist, but the smears and oblique approaches from Whitehall were always rejected at PHS. One tongue-in-cheek response was that I was a Basque, and therefore against all forms of government. It was thought just as well that I was not stationed in London.

Perhaps, but above all I was a Cockney. I had lived at the bottom of the heap too long to accept unquestioningly the attitudes and prejudices of those at the top. *The Times* may be the paper of Top People, but it was among the first to recognize postwar change and tried honestly to report the consequences. Perhaps the then editors saw me as a representative of change. I may have come quickly to terms with Britain's reduced circumstances after the war because my circumstances had always been reduced (that's a lark!), but Cockney realism made me a better reporter. I would like to think that Cockney humour and humanity also helped. The first certainly made life more enjoyable.

On balance, I am glad that I was born a Cockney. I do not see moral merit in poverty as such. It is not uplifting to live without a bathroom. I may have missed a great deal, but I had a happy childhood. This book, written as honestly as I know how, should be sufficient proof. Shadwell could be a squalid place, but generally speaking Cockneys are one of the nicest and most civilized groups I have ever met. This can be held to be a sentimental view. Perhaps it is. Sentimentality is a Cockney weakness, but they have the qualities of groups conditioned but not brutalized by poverty. Professor Jacques Barzun once wrote, with reference to the descendants of the huge waves of immigrants to the United States at about the turn of the century, that the American majority were the prosperous poor. They had inherited from the European poor a diffused amiability, a restraint in social intercourse, and an inbred recognition that they must live together and had best be pleasant to one another.

The average Cockney is, or was, certainly amiable, moderate and unassuming. His fortitude had a monumental dignity, but humour was always a happy relief. His ability to adjust to yet another misfortune or injustice was probably unprecedented, but he had a strong sense of justice and fair play. He knew how to enjoy life. He had a culture of his own no less real because anthropologists prefer to investigate growing up in Samoa or other processes of little relevance to industrial and post-industrial societies. He was a true urban creature, perhaps the oldest in the world. The culture which emerged from his extraordinary circumstances is dimly reflected in old music hall songs such as, *Knocked them in the Old Kent Road*, *I'm one of the ruins Cromwell knocked about a bit* and even *My old Dutch*. They were a very considerable people, but they carried the seeds of their own destruction. They were too amiable, too moderate and too unassuming. They had too strong a sense of fair play, and trusted too much in the well meaning of others.

As with the poor everywhere they were put upon. No government or party really cared about them. The do-gooders never appreciated their worth. Yet they performed a distinctive and historic role. They gave London its special flavour, which still sets it apart from other great cities. London stands supreme not because of Big Ben, red buses and plane trees, theatres and parks, but because the Cockneys, more than any other group, know that they must live together and had best be pleasant to one another. They successfully and uncomplainingly absorbed the hordes of immigrants from Ireland with their bog priests and eastern European Jews with forbidding appearance and social and religious exlusiveness. Judging from the literature of the period, it could be argued that they were the only English social group more or less free of anti-Semitism. The processes of assimilation worked both ways. Cockney humour is partly Jewish humour. The two are largely self protective, and each has strengthened the other. There can't be a more typical Cockney than a Jewish Cockney. They also took the brunt of the bombing in the second world war. *London can take it* was the heroic claim during the blitz, and it was true. But not because of Churchill sitting safe in his underground bunker, or the well-to-do evacuees sweating it out in the country, or suburbanites living in safe areas and with air-raid shelters in their back gardens. The Cockneys took it, living in the bullseye of the *Luftwaffe's* main target and with only a few underground stations and their own fortitude for protection.

None of this has ever been recognized. The fieldmarshals and admirals were well taken care of after the war but the Cockneys were not even given their due. The New Park was created in memory of King Edward the Seventh, but nothing was done to commemorate Cockney courage in the blitz. Instead, so-called planners set out to destroy what had survived the bombing. In their ignorant arrogance they destroyed the conditions of Cockney culture, the tight little neighbourhoods, the street markets, the intimate pubs and the corner shops. Almost nothing is now left of Watney Street. If I still lived in Shadwell I would have to walk more than a mile to do my shopping. Then the Cockneys were expected to absorb Pakistani immigrants by middle-class liberals living miles from the smell of their cooking, and were condemned as racists when a few complained. The Paleseum now only shows Indian and Pakistani films. Even their main livelihood has been taken away, and again they were condemned for fighting for survival in the only way they know how—by militant industrial action at the container yard gates. One can argue that industry must be rationalized if Britain is to prosper. I suppose a case can even be made for tower blocks, but when everything has been said the brutal fact will remain that Cockney life has been killed and largely by indifference and contempt. There is an old Cockney song with the refrain, *Ain't it all a bloody shame*. Well, it is, and not only for the East End. Cockneys had something to offer, the ability to live peacefully and happily in a crowded urban environment. Its passing will be regretted one of these days.

But I do not want to end on a sour note. That would be most unCockney. It would also be misleading. Remnants of the old life survive among the tower blocks. People are still nice to each other and strangers. Pakistanis have a better chance of being accepted in the East End than elsewhere. As for those who have moved on or have been moved, I meet them, the new Diaspora, everywhere, and not only in buses